OTHELLO

WILLIAM SHAKESPEARE

PEACOCK BOOKS

Published by
PEACOCK BOOKS
7/22, Ansari Road, Darya Ganj, New Delhi-110002
Phones : +91-11-40775252, 40775214, 23273880, 23275880
Fax : +91-11-23285873
Web : www.atlanticbooks.com
E-mail : orders@atlanticbooks.com

Peacock Books is an imprint of
Atlantic Publishers and Distributors (P) Ltd

First published 1622

Printed & bound in India by Atlantic Print Services

CONTENTS

SHAKESPEARE'S PLAYS WITH THEIR PROBABLE APPROXIMATE DATES

There is absence of total agreement on the dates of Shakespearean plays. Some scholars give an earlier date than the one suggested here for Shakespeare's first play. Doubt also remains concerning the actual order of composition in particular years. Having stated that, the editor gives hereunder the approximate dates as largely accepted by Shakespeare scholars in general.

1590-91
Henry VI Part II
Henry VI Part III

1591-92
Henry VI Part I

1592-93
Richard III
Comedy of Errors

1593-94
Titus Andronicus
Taming of the Shrew

1594-95
Two Gentlemen of Verona
Love's Labour's Lost
Romeo and Juliet

1595-96
Richard II
Midsummer Night's Dream

1596-97
King John
Merchant of Venice

1597-98
Henry IV Part I
Henry IV Part II

1598-99
Much Ado About Nothing
Henry V

1599-1600
Julius Caesar
As You Like It
Twelfth Night

1600-1601
Hamlet
Merry Wives of Windsor

1601-02
Troilus and Cressida

1602-03
All is Well That Ends Well

1604-05
Measure for Measure
Othello

1605-06
King Lear
Macbeth

1606-07
Antony and Cleopatra

1607-08
Coriolanus
Timon of Athens

1608-09
Pericles

1609-10
Cymbeline

1610-11
Winter's Tale

1611-12
The Tempest

1612-13
Henry VIII
Two Noble Kinsmen

WILLIAM SHAKESPEARE

BIOGRAPHICAL SKETCH

1. A Symbol of Culture

Introducing Shakespeare to the general reader, G.B. Harrison begins his book with the following statement:

> No household in the English-speaking world is properly furnished unless it contains copies of the *Holy Bible* and of *The Works of William Shakespeare.* It is not always thought necessary that these books should be read in maturer years, but they must be present as symbols of Religion and Culture.

Not only in the English speaking world, but everywhere, acquaintance with Shakespeare's plays is regarded as a mark of culture; and there is hardly any language-community in the civilized world, which does not possess Shakespeare in translation.

2. Life

Anyone looking for reliable historical information about Shakespeare is bound to meet with disappointment. We get very little help from his contemporaries in the form of recorded reference allusion, or memoirs, Shakespeare himself is completely silent about himself, and as regards his works, he has consumed himself into them so perfectly that it is very risky to draw any clear inferences from his works—except, perhaps, the sonnets, some of which, departing from the convention, appear to be expressing personal experience. We do, however, get some definite information from the parish register, legal documents and town records.

At first sight, it may appear astonishing that such a great writer as Shakespeare should have received no notice from his contemporaries and that no attempt should have been made to preserve every bit of the records associated with his life. But a second look at the state of affairs and attitude to biography prevailing in that period will mollify our uneasiness. The Elizabethans, generally, were indifferent to biographical and autobiographical notes and memoirs; even the biography of the most important personage, Queen Elizabeth herself, is full of gaps and guesses. It should, in fact, be gratifying that we possess more of authentic information about Shakespeare than about any of his contemporary writers excepting Ben Jonson. Moreover, Shakespeare, until very late in his life, was a very ordinary individual belonging to the socially unwelcome profession of actor; and the playwrights, too, were not much distinguished in the society. The critical response to his work was not unmixed high praise until the end of the eighteenth century. It was only in the beginning of the nineteenth century that Shakespeare became established as a great writer who must be spoken of with a feeling of reverence. But during the intervening centuries, he had been steadily moving towards the highest position, and as this process advanced, his admirers became over enthusiastic to complete his biography. The result was an infusion of a great deal of guesswork aggrandisement and romanticising. In such a situation, the best policy will be to keep close to the attested facts and reasonable inferences, except in cases where a highly dubious anecdote may, nevertheless, indicate some important turn in the dramatist's life.

William Shakespeare—the surname is found spelled in various other ways, which was not unusual in those days—was the son of John Shakespeare of Stratford-on-Avon. In 1556 John Shakespeare bought a house in Henley Street. In 1552, he, along with two neighbours, had been fined for keeping an unauthorized dunghill on Henley Street, which means he had been dwelling there for some years before he bought the house. In 1557 he married Mary Arden, the daughter of Robert Arden, a land-owning farmer who lived in Wilmcote, a small village two miles from Stratford. Mary brought with her an inheritance of sixty acres of land.

John Shakespeare was a glove-maker and dealer in wool, he may have at one time or another, pursued some other trades as well. He was a prosperous citizen of Stratford and one of its notables.

In the year of William Shakespeare's birth, however, his father was a prosperous businessman who was also a man of substance and of social standing. William, the third and surviving child of John and Mary Shakespeare was baptized on 26 April 1564. Allowing the usual period of three days between birth and baptism, it is generally assumed that William Shakespeare was born on 23 April 1564, which is also the day of the feast of St. George, the patron saint of England—and this is also the day on which Shakespeare breathed his last. The Shakespeares had five more children. It requires no documentary evidence to say that Shakespeare during his childhood observed and absorbed the life of town and village surging all around him and, possessing a rare talent, he stored in his mind sights, sounds, scenes and characters, which, combined with his experience of London, would prove a rich material at the forge of his creativity, when he came to write poems and plays.

There is no valid reason to doubt that William was enrolled in the local grammar school when he was six or seven years old. His father was still a prominent citizen and an important member of the borough council. But the school records for the period are not available. Nicholas Rowe, who brought out the first edited collection of Shakespeare's plays, wrote in his introduction that the boy studied in a free school where "it is probable, he acquired what Latin he was master of, but the narrowness of his circumstances, and the want of his assistance at home, forced his father to withdraw him from thence, and unhappily prevented his further proficiency in that language". John Aubrey a seventeenth-century antiquarian and biographer, in his *Brief Lives* published posthumously in 1813, informs us that Shakespeare had been a school master in a country school.

There is, however, no confusion regarding his early marriage to Anne Hathaway, who was about eight years his senior. One thing that can be safely inferred is that Shakespeare was an impetuous and highly romantic young man and this conclusion gets ample support in the essential nature of all his writings—they are romantic through and through. On 26th May 1583, their first issue Susanna was baptized in Stratford and two years later, the twins, Hamnet and Judith were born and christened on 2 February 1585. Of these children of Shakespeare, Hamnet died in 1596, Susanna married a physician named John Hall and inherited a major portion of her father's assets, Judith married Thomas Quiney.

The period from 1585 to 1592 in Shakespeare's life is known as the "dark years" or "lost years" from the biographer's point of view. For this period we have no authentic information about the family apart from a single reference to John Shakespeare in 1588 in connection with a legal dispute over a sum of money. There is, however, no dearth of legend and hearsay. According to Nicholas Rowe, Shakespeare incurred the wrath of the local landlord, Sir Thomas Lucy for stealing deer in his park and was, as a result, obliged to flee to London.

Though there are many conjectures, yet what sounds most credible is that Shakespeare attached himself to one of the touring theatrical companies that visited the countryside during the period under consideration. Three such companies, the Earl of Worcester's Men, the Earl of Oxford's Men and the Earl of Essex's Men, were giving performances at Stratford in 1581 and in 1585 the town people were entertained by an unidentified company. In 1587, the year in which Shakespeare most probably left his home town, the Earl of Essex's Men and the Earl of Leicester's Men were in Stratford; he might have accompanied one of these groups to London.

In the midst of financial and other problems besetting the family, joining a company of actors must have appealed to Shakespeare as a good expedient because it would bring some wages as well as give him an access to the literary world of London.

By 1592 Shakespeare's struggle had begun to bear fruit; in that year he was worthy enough to arouse the jealousy of another playwright, Robert Greene, one of the University Wits. In a letter addressed to his fellow writers and appended to a pamphlet called *Greene's Groatsworth of Wit Bought with a Million of Repentance* he made a scurrilous attack on Shakespeare for presuming to be not only an actor but the best playwright.

It is clear that by 1592 Shakespeare had established himself in London as an actor and dramatist: he had completed at least the three plays comprising the *Henry VI* trilogy; he had also probably been improving and retouching existing plays and there might have been some talk of his writing then in progress. Some scholars have argued that he had also completed or was about to complete *The Two Gentlemen of Verona, The Comedy of Errors, The Taming of the Shrew, Richard III, Titus Andronicus* and *Love's Labour's Lost.*

The next year, 1593, saw the publication of a long narrative poem, *Venus and Adonis*, with a signed dedication to Henry Wriothesley, the third Earl of Southampton: "Your Honour's in all duty, William Shakespeare". In the following year came out another poem, *The Rape of Lucrece*, also dedicated to the same lord. This was the period during which the London theatres remained closed on account of the plague; that Shakespeare did not waste his time, but was busy writing poetry shows with what earnestness he pursued his aim of achieving literary renown. He had also started writing his sonnets during this period and some scholars have suggested that the group of sonnets addressed to a young man had the Earl of Southampton for their inspirator.

The theatres reopened in 1594 and staging of plays including some by Shakespeare began. We find that he is already an important member of Lord Chamberlain's company as disclosed by the following entry in the Chamber Accounts:

> To William Kemp, William Shakespeare, and Richard Burbage, servants to the Lord Chamberlain, upon the Council's warrant dated at Whitehall 15 March 1594 (-5) for two several

> comedies or interludes showed by them before her Majesty in Christmas time last past, *viz.* upon St. Stephen's day and Innocent's day, £ 13 6s, 8d, and by way of her Majesty's reward £ 6 13s, 4d.

From recorded references, allusions and lists of actors prefixed to printed plays, we gather that Shakespeare continued to act on the stage at least up to 1603 and if we rely on his fellow-actors, John Heminge and Henry Condell, who edited the First Folio edition of his plays in 1623, up to 1611. He is said to have played kingly roles including the Ghost in *Hamlet* but he also acted the part of old servant Adam in *As You Like It*. According to Aubrey, he "did act exceedingly well".

All the while Shakespeare was making steady progress in writing plays and in earning money and fame. During 1595-96, five of his new plays were produced: *Richard II*, *Romeo and Juliet*, *King John*, *A Midsummer Night's Dream*, and *The Merchant of Venice*. During the latter year there was a tragedy in the family: his only son Hamnet died in August 1596. In the same year, there was some more trouble for Shakespeare: according to a reference discovered by Leslie Hotson in 1931, one William Wayt claimed sureties of the peace against William Shakespeare and some other persons including Francis Langley then owner of the Swan Theatre. But his financial position was quite sound. He was living in a large house in Bishopsgate as the tax-rolls indicate, perhaps his family also stayed with him for brief periods. There is evidence of his purchase of property in London and in his hometown.

While living in London, Shakespeare appears to have maintained good links with his native place and its people. His narrative poems had been printed by Richard Field who had migrated from Stratford. In 1597 Shakespeare bought the largest house in Stratford, called New Place, from William Underhill for a sum of £ 60. On October 25, 1598, Richard Quiney a Stratford man who was visiting London wrote a letter to Shakespeare requesting a loan of £ 30. In 1599 the famous actor, Richard Burbage and his brother Cuthbert set up a new playhouse on the Bankside, called the Globe. Since they could not finance the project on their own, they invited some other members of their company, Lord Chamberlain's Men, to become shareholders. Shakespeare thus became a part-owner of the Globe, entitled to ten per cent of the profits. He enjoyed the unique privilege of being a dramatist, actor and businessman.

During the period 1597-99 six more plays comprising comedies and plays on English history were produced: *Merry Wives of Windsor, Much Ado About Nothing, As You Like It, Henry IV-Part One, Henry IV-Part Two,* and *Henry V,* probably *Julius Caesar* also had its first staging in 1599.

The new century opened with a personal tragedy to Shakespeare: his father died in 1601. It also brought him to the threshold of his tragic vision—the truest and profoundest ever presented to theatre audiences and to the readers of the world. Before the death of Queen Elizabeth in 1603, the greatest tragedy of personal dilemma *Hamlet* had its first performance. His finest comedy, *Twelfth Night* and the 'problem play' *Troilus and Cressida* were also produced before 1603. With the accession of King James to the English throne, Lord Chamberlain's Men, evidently regarded as the best company of actors, was taken under royal patronage and was renamed King's Men. The letters patent issued on 19 May 1603 mention William Shakespeare along with some other members of the company including Heminge and Condell, the future editors of the first edition of his Collected Plays. The actors of the company became eligible to special privileges; records indicate that they were often called upon to present plays before the Court and to participate in royal pageants and processions—several Shakespeare plays were performed at the Court. In March 1604, when King James made a 'royal proceeding' through the city of London, Shakespeare—as well as each of his fellow players—was given four yards of red cloth for his livery.

On the plane of worldly affairs too, Shakespeare was faring very well. In May 1602 he purchased one hundred and seven acres of arable land to the parish of old Stratford and in September he acquired a cottage in Chapel Lane, Stratford-on-Avon. A fellow actor, Augustine Phillipps, when he made his will in May 1605, mentioned Shakespeare first among the recipients of his bequests of gold pieces: "I give and bequeath to my fellow, William Shakespeare, a thirty-shilling piece in gold." Two years later in 1607 his favourite daughter Susanna, married the physician John Hall and in February 1608 their daughter Elizabeth was born. It is almost certain that Edmond Shakespeare whose burial is recorded in the registers of the Church of St. Saviours in Southwark was the poet's brother. Shakespeare's mother died in 1608.

In Shakespeare's literary output, the period 1604-1608 is the period of great tragedies: *Othello, Macbeth, King Lear, Antony and Cleopatra* and *Cariolanus.* The other plays first produced during this period are: *Measure for Measure, All is Well That Ends Well* and *Timon of Athens.* Some scholars, however, believe that *All* is *Well That Ends Well* is an early play, perhaps *Love's Labour's Won*, mentioned by Francis Meres in his *Palladis Tamia* (1598).

In 1608 the King's Men took over the Blackfriars, an indoor theatre where Henry Evans's children's company had been staging plays since 1600. Shakespeare thus began writing plays for both Blackfriars and the Globe. He appears to have adjusted himself to the conditions and upper-class audiences at the Blackfriars. Otherwise, too, Shakespeare about this time had emerged from the Inferno of human and supernatural evil. He had explored the genesis, nature, working and consequences of evil and expressed them in the best of utterance. Now in the last phase of his career, he turned to superior kinds of solutions. Evil keeps raising its head, but it is confronted by higher human nature and is overthrown without waste or destruction. This is the tenor of his last plays: *Pericles, Cymbeline, The Winter's Tale, The Tempest.*

William Shakespeare had made his life a grand success: Whatever wrongs, malice, envy or injury he had suffered were behind him; he had become rich and respected; thousands of human hearts had been moved to laughter and tears by the magic of his lines; he had learnt the last lesson in human wisdom.

Around 1611 Shakespeare contentedly retired to Stratford. His remaining two younger brothers, Gilbert and Richard died in 1612 and 1613 respectively. John Combe, one of his closest friends also died in 1613 leaving him a bequest of £ 5. On March 10, 1613, he bought the Blackfriar's Gate House.

Shakespeare did not break his relations completely with his company; he also kept visiting London from time to time. The last two plays which he wrote in collaboration with John Fletcher are *Henry VII* and *The Two Noble Kinsmen*, but his heart wasn't there; they suffer in execution and in imaginative power. Shakespeare's health began to deteriorate after 1613. According to one report some time in 1616 Drayton and Ben Jonson came down to visit him and they had a merry meeting. His will was drawn up in January 1616. Since his younger daughter Judith got married to Thomas Quiney on February 10, the will was revised and executed by him on March 25.

In his will, Shakespeare bequeathed nearly all his property to his elder daughter Susanna Hall and her husband; Judith his younger daughter received very little in comparison. Perhaps Shakespeare was not happy with Judith's marriage to Thomas Quiney about whom there was some scandal, or, he feared any fixed assets made over to her would not remain secure, but he made provision for yearly payment of some money to her. This apparent lack of balance on the part of Shakespeare is bound to remind us of his own creation *King Lear*.

Another matter which causes surprise is the bequest to his wife. She is not mentioned by name and Shakespeare appears to have added one sentence about her as an after thought: "I give unto my wife my second best bed with the furniture". Those who defend Shakespeare on this issue argue that the best bed in the house would be reserved for guests, that he gave her the second best bed because it carried past associations since this must have been the bed the couple used to sleep in. It is also true that Anne's dower rights already stood protected bylaw; she must have continued to live in New Place until her death in 1623. And yet, when all this has been said, one cannot help feeling that this slighting gesture on the part of Shakespeare indicates that something had gone sour in their relations.

He left something to each of his relations: niece Elizabeth Hall, sister Joan and her three sons; he did not forget his friends and the poor of Stratford, to whom he bequeathed ten pounds. It is to be noted that he gave 26s. 8d. each to his former fellow actors, John Heminge, Richard Burbage and Henry Condell for buying mourning rings.

Shakespeare died on 23 April, 1616, but Death could not be proud of this, for in black ink his name still shines bright. A monument representing the poet in the act of writing with a quill was installed some time between his death and the year 1623. This is the famous bust with which the whole world has become familiar. The other authentic likeness is Martin Droeshout's engraving on the title page of the First Folio Collection of Shakespeare's Plays, which is equally familiar to readers. The epitaph inscribed under the bust praises Shakespeare as a writer.

With whome
Quick nature died; whose name doth deck
this tombe
Far more than most, sith all that He hath writt
Leaves living art, but page, to serve his witt.

OTHELLO

A CRITICAL INTRODUCTION

(i) DATE OF COMPOSITION AND SOURCE

Date: Even though the date of composition cannot be fixed with absolute certainty, the more generally accepted belief is that *Othello* was written in, or about the year 1604. There is an entry showing that the King's players acted a play called *The Moor of Venice* before the Court of King James I on the first of November, 1604. This is the earliest reference to the play which was then probably not more than two years old.

Source: Shaw, once accused Shakespeare of never having attempted to write an 'original' play. By 'original', he perhaps meant a play of which the author had invented the plot for himself. However this idea of originality is of rather a recent origin. The story of the Moor of Venice, *Un Captiano Moro*, was published in 1566 in a collection of such stories, entitled, *Hecatomithi*. The author was Giraldi Cinthio. However it is doubtful whether Shakespeare had access to a translation of the work cited. It is possible that he heard the story and artistically used it for his own purpose. However there are significant changes in the two versions. According to Cinthio, the whole plot hinges on an ensign's passion for Desdemona. Shakespeare's answer to this is the character of Iago. Shakespeare has also affected significant changes in the character of Iago. He makes Othello a heroic figure, worthy of tragedy. Othello is presented so as to win the audience's sympathy. Moreover rather than facing punishment as a common murderer, he is made to end his own life by Shakespeare.

(ii) INTRODUCTION

Othello is the only play which appeared in quarto in 1622 in the interval between Shakespeare's death and the publication of the first folio. We have no means, except by internal evidence of ascertaining the date when the play was written. Upon the strength of a supposed allusion to the armorial bearings of the new order of Baronets, instituted in 1611 (Act III; Scene iv; lines 46-47) the play has been referred to a year not earlier than 1611; but the metrical tests confirm the impression produced by the general character and spirit of the tragedy, that it cannot belong to the same period as *The Tempest*, *Cymbeline* and *The Winter's Tale*. It is evidently one of the group of tragedies of passion which includes *Macbeth* and *Lear*. The year 1604 has been accepted by several critics as a not improbable date for *Othello*.

The original of the story is found in Cinthio's *Hecatomithi*, but it has been in a marvellous manner elevated and recreated by Shakespeare. Coleridge has justly said that the agonized doubt contrasts Othello with Leontes in *The Winter's Tale*, and Leonatus in *Cymbeline*. A mean watchfulness or prime suspicion is the last thing that Othello could be guilty of. He is of a free and noble nature, naturally trustful, with a kind of grand innocence, retaining some of his barbaric simpleness of soul in midst of the subtle and astute politicians of Venice. He is great in simple heroic action, but unversed in the complex affairs of life, and a stranger to the malignant deceits of the debased Italian character. Nothing is more chivalrous, more romantic than the lore of Othello and Desdemona. The beautiful Italian girl is fascinated by the real strength and grandeur, and the render protectiveness of the Moor. He is charmed by the sweetness, the sympathy, the gentle disposition, the gracious womanliness of Desdemona. But neither quite rightly knows the other; there is none of that perfect equality and perfect knowledge between them which unite so flawlessly Brutus and Portia. There is no character in Shakespeare's plays so full of serpentine power and serpentine poison as Iago. He is envious of Cassio and suspects that the Moor may have wronged his honour; but his malignancy is out of all proportion to even its alleged motives. Cassio, notwithstanding his moral weaknesses, is of a chivalrous nature, possessed by enthusiastic admiration of his great general and the beautiful lady who is his wife. But Iago can see neither human virtue nor greatness. All things to him are common and unclean, and he is content that they should be so. He is not the sly, sneaking and too manifest villain of some of the actors of his part. He is "honest Iago" and passes for a rough yet shrewd critic of life, who is himself frank and candid. To ensnare the nobly guileless Othello was, therefore, no impossible task. Shakespeare does not allow Iago to triumph; his end is wretched as his life has been. And Othello, restored to love through such tragic calamity, dies once more reunited to his wife, and loyal, in spite of all his wrongs, to the city of his adoption. It is he who has sinned, and not she who was dearer to him than himself, and of his own wrongs and griefs he can make a sudden end.

(iii) ACTWISE SUMMARY OF THE PLAY

Act I

Brabantio, a rich senator of Venice, has a fair daughter named Desdemona. Othello, a black Moor, is a brave soldier who has risen to the rank of the general in the Venetian army. Desdemona loves the stories of travel and adventure, related by Othello and eventually falls in love with him. Othello proposes to her and she privately consents to marry him. Despite being an admirer of Othello, Brabantio cannot accept him as his son-in-law. He accuses the Moor of having seduced his fair daughter by spells of magic and witchcraft.

Venice is threatened by a Turkish fleet which is heading towards the island of Cyprus. Othello had established Venetian supremacy over the Turks in previous wars but now in this hour of crisis, Othello is being charged as an offender by Brabantio. The senate gives the old and respected senator a most patient hearing but the Duke, who acted as chief judge, is greatly impressed by Othello's tale of love, related in a plain and truthful discourse. Desdemona, too, appears and talks of her duty to her father as well as her greater duty to her lord and master, Othello. The old senator ultimately has to withdraw, bestowing on Othello his fair daughter in marriage.

Othello now undertakes the management of the war against the Turks.

Act II

Landing in Cyprus with Desdemona, Othello learns of the dispersion of the Turkish fleet because of a storm. Since the threat of war has receded, everyone is in a mood of merry-making. Iago, a capable soldier, has all along nurtured ill-will against Cassio who has been made the lieutenant by Othello, ignoring Iago who had a better claim. Cassio has been close to both Othello and Desdemona for he had acted as a go between in the love affair of the two. Now Iago thinks of bringing Cassio as well as Othello to discomfiture for having wronged him. Cassio has been assigned duty as an officer by Othello to ensure that soldiers do not misbehave and cause disorder in the island. Iago entices Cassio to make rather too free with the bottle. Now Cassio is not in control of himself. Iago has arranged that Roderigo would provoke Cassio and the plan succeeds. There is a scuffle and Montano is injured in the fracas. When Othello discovers it, he has no option but to fire Cassio. Cassio is most repentant. Iago now advises him to seek Desdemona's help in winning back Othello's trust.

Act III

As instructed Cassio sought Desdemona's help and she promised to talk to Othello. Othello is persuaded by her to receive Cassio again in favour but after a while. As Cassio is leaving Desdemona's chamber, Othello and Iago happen to enter it. But knitting his brow and by murmuring something under his breath, Iago arouses Othello's suspicion against Desdemona. Appearing most reluctant to talk about this, Iago suggests persuasively to Othello that Desdemona is capable of deceiving others, for she deceived her own father by marrying Othello. She is headstrong. There is something unnatural about her, for she chose to marry a Moor, discarding so many other suitable matches of her clime and complexion. Very cleverly Iago suggests that Desdemona now has a preference for Cassio. He further advises Othello to put off his reconciliation with Cassio a little longer and to see with what earnestness Desdemona intercedes on his behalf.

Othello loses his cool at all this. He catches Iago by the throat and demands proof of what he is alleging. Iago saves himself by claiming that he had seen Cassio wipe his face with a certain handkerchief, spotted with strawberries, that he (Othello) had given to her as a token of love. Othello promises to devise some suitable means of her death, if it is like that.

Act IV

Iago further poisons Othello's mind against Desdemona and Cassio by feeding his suspicions. Othello is so excited and incensed that he faints, Iago fears that a meeting between Cassio and Othello may lead to his exposure and so he sends Cassio away. Iago then asks Othello to hide himself and watch a conversation between Cassio and himself to have a proof of Desdemona's falseness. Iago talks to Cassio about Bianca but cleverly avoids mentioning her name. Othello, being out of earshot supposes that they are talking of Desdemona and that Cassio's mirth is inspired by the tale of his conquest. Bianca enters and angrily returns Desdemona's handkerchief to Cassio, believing it to be a love token from some other woman. Othello is convinced that it is his handkerchief. In great anger, Iago suggests that he should strangle Desdemona in her bed she has contaminated. He goes to her but a Senate representative arrives with a letter for him. Desdemona innocently is pursuing still her plea for Cassio's reinstatement "out of her love for Cassio". Othello strikes her in the presence of the Senate ambassador. Othello meets Emilia and cross-examines her regarding Cassio's relations with Desdemona. He does not believe her protestations regarding his wife's fidelity. He treats Emilia most shabbily and abuses her. He calls Desdemona 'a whore' at her face. She is very much hurt. She asks Emilia to lay on her bed her wedding sheets. She calls "good Iago" to seek her advice. He dismisses Othello's strange conduct as his humour.

Roderigo complains to Iago of his neglect. He threatens to expose Iago. Iago, alarmed, seeks to buy his silence by engaging him to murder Cassio.

Act V

Iago is determined to get rid of both Cassio and Roderigo for his safety. Cassio is attacked by Roderigo, as instructed, but he hits back and injures Roderigo. Iago also comes from behind and injures Cassio in the leg. Othello hears Cassio's cries and feels content that 'good Iago' has attempted to punish his wife's seducer. Iago now enters and stabs Roderigo for having attempted to murder Cassio.

Othello rushes to Desdemona's chamber to strangle her. He keeps on reminding himself that it is just punishment for her conduct. He cannot help kissing her several times. He asks her to prepare her soul for heaven by confessing her sins but she insists on her innocence. She denies Othello's vile charge and asks him to call Cassio to vouch for her. But Othello is obstinate, he considers her protestations but attempts to befoul him. He strangles her. Just then Emilia enters. The dying Desdemona tells her that she herself has done it but Othello confesses his crime. He explains that his wife was guilty of adultery with Cassio and Iago can vouch for it. But Emilia calls Iago a liar. She exposes Iago and completely by revealing that she had taken the handkerchief from Desdemona. Othello runs at Iago who stabs his wife and runs away. But he is captured. Cassio is also brought in a chair. Othello, in anger, wounds Iago with a sword. Letters received from Roderigo's dead body are explained by Cassio and the whole plot exposed. Othello is now convinced of Cassio's innocence. Othello, in extreme repentance stabs himself. He asks the Senate messengers to explain his conduct to the Senate. Cassio, the new Governor, is left with the task of punishing the 'spartan dog' Iago.

(iv) CHARACTERS IN THE PLAY

(a) Othello

Othello is perhaps the most romantic of Shakespeare's heroes. He has lived a life full of most unimaginable adventures, having met marvellous people, cannibals, the anthropophagi and other strange, incredible persons. He has been chased, caught and sold as a slave. He has had hair-breadth escapes. He seems to bear a charmed life. He is brave, valiant, 'all in all sufficient'.

Othello is noble, respectable, magnanimous, self-controlled and last but not least humble, poised and lacking in arrogance. However he is also simple, guileless and trustful. He is not observant or capable of probing into the minds of men. When once his suspicions are aroused, he must ascertain the truth without loss of time. When once he is convinced and determines his course of action, he has no hesitation whatsoever in carrying it through to the end. He lacks practical wisdom and is conscious of his lack. It is therefore that he takes Iago for his guide and he depends on him entirely. Likewise he centres everything on his love of Desdemona to the extent that when he is convinced that she is false to him, his whole universe goes into a spin. His sense of honour and his poet's ideal of love are mortally offended. And he holds it as a solemn duty imposed on him to see that Desdemona pays the penalty of this offence. When this 'gull' and 'dolt' is told the truth by Emilia, his sense of justice is revolted again and it is only by punishing himself that he thinks he can restore order.

(b) Iago

A professional soldier, Iago feels disappointed when Cassio is preferred. His absolute egoism is hurt and his monstrous intellectual force gets employed to teach Othello a lesson. Othello and Cassio's 'overfamiliarity' with his wife, Emilia, also rouses his ire. Iago's blunt and rough ways make him hate Cassio's courtier's manners. He also feels jealous of Othello's great openness and trustfulness of nature. The cynic in him ridicules love, virtue, beauty and moral values. Since he cannot be Othello's match in fame, grace and social position, he comes to be contemptuous of all these as worthless.

Iago's conceit and self-love make him incapable of loving anyone except himself. He does not love Desdemona, for it is he who suggests the manner of her murder. Even earlier he had remained unmoved upon her distress at the end of Act IV; Scene (ii). It is the sadistic instinct in him which makes him behave like that, especially with regard to one whose love he cannot win for himself. He deliberately presents himself as outspoken and Iago out of the sheer nobility of his soul, comes to trust him as a 'rough diamond' who is 'no-nonsense' and 'honest'.

Despite being what he is, it is by sheer chance that things take the shape they do in the play. Iago had originally intended to sow the seeds of suspicion in Othello's mind about Desdemona and to take Cassio's place. But as the situation unfolds, Iago, the master dissimulator goes along, never letting the situation get the better of him. What motives does he have for acting thus? All his reasons for his actions are thought up after the event. This demi-devil is always trying to give himself reason for his malignity. Coleridge aptly describes Iago's reflections as 'the motive hunting of a motiveless malignity'.

Iago, however, is not without another dimension to his being. He compels a certain grudging admiration for his cool-headedness, his fearsome ability to appear always in control, his quick-witted cleverness, his ever-ready armoury of strategy and tactics to wriggle out of any situation. Iago seems a formidable adversary, sheer unscrupulous reason let loose.

(c) Desdemona

Desdemona is simplicity personified. She cannot even imagine the existence of evil. When accused of being a 'whore' by Othello, she can only pathetically ask, "Am I—that name, Iago?" It is because of this innocent purity that she suffers a tragic fate. Rightly has she been described as "gentleness in its excess, gentleness verging on passiveness".

Desdemona is also unworldly, guileless and tactless. Even when she realizes that all was not well with Othello's temper, she continues to press Cassio's suit. The reason perhaps is her innocent love for Othello—unselfish, tender, trusting and self-effacing. Her love also has an admixture of fear:

> "And yet I fear you, for you are fatal then
> When your eyes roll so"

It is this fear of Othello, combined with his story of the supernatural that makes her tell a lie about the lost handkerchief. However when Othello accuses her most heartlessly, she behaves in a most dignified manner, not with loud and weeping protest. She prepares for her death but is indifferent to her fate, until, at the last minute, she pleads for mercy and protests her innocence. The only other lie we wear from her lips is the final proof of her unchanged love for Othello. When Emilia asks her "Who hath done this deed?", referring to her being suffocated to death, Desdemona replies:

"Nobody. I myself...farewell.

Commend me to my kind lord. Oh—farewell". What Emilia exclaims sums up her character well:

"Oh she was heavenly true !"

(d) Emilia

Emilia is an important character in the play helping to bring closer the happenings which lead to tragedy. This waiting woman of Desdemona's is a foil to her mistress. Unlike Desdemona, she is cynical and sour, the result of her having married Othello. To Desdemona's query "Would you commit a foul sin for all the world?" her matter-of-fact answer is: "Who would not make her husband a cuckold to make him a monarch?" Her commonsense is in striking contrast to Desdemona's angelic purity. It is by putting the two characters together that the readers can see the two extremes heightened.

Like Desdemona, Emilia too is a big afraid of her husband. In the matter of the handkerchief, she lends herself stupidly, but innocently to Iago's purpose. When Othello calls for it, and Desdemona is in distress for its loss, Emilia, who could have explained the matter in a moment, remains silent in dread of her husband. Bradley considers her stupidity in the matter as gross but it is stupidity and nothing worse, according to him. There is no ground for suspecting that she is aware of Iago's plot and plays into his hands. She feels that somebody is cozening Othello but she suspects nobody in particular. Shakespeare also gives us every reason to believe that she was completely deceived in him. Her amazed, thrice repeated "My husband makes that clear". In the case of the handkerchief, she gives way unwillingly and pleads feebly to have it returned to "the poor lady" who will "run mad" when she misses it. But when she hears (for she has been listening at the door) Othello abusing Desdemona, her anger breaks out against the slanderer who has abused the Moor.

A hidden facet of Emilia's character is revealed when she sees Desdemona dead. She flames into a passion of indignant grief. She turns like a tigress on Othello and reviles him for his guilt and folly. When her loyalty to her husband, Iago clashes with her loyalty to her mistress, she is in no confusion whatsoever. She scorns to be silent.

> "I peace?
> No, I will peak as liberal as the north."

Fearless of "heaven, and men and devils," she champions her dead mistress's purity. And so echoing with her last breath, her mistress's willow song, she dies in music. She sacrifices her life for her mistress's good name. Dr. Bradley aptly remarks: "Nothing in her life became her like the losing it." Another critic, Granville-Barker opines, "Emilia has won herself a place in the play's tragic heaven."

(v) IS JEALOUSY OTHELLO'S TRAGIC FLAW?

Bradley has put forth the view that Shakespeare's tragic heroes are exceptional men both in status and character traits but they have one single tragic flaw which may be insignificant in itself but given the circumstances in which the hero is placed, it proves to be crucial and fatal, paving the way for the protagonist's fall and destruction. Macbeth is 'ambitious', Hamlet is indecisive and in their particular situations these attributes lead to their doom. In case of Othello, 'jealousy' is said to be the tragic flaw.

The play certainly leaves, at one level, the impression that Othello has been put

> "At least into a jealousy so strong
> That judgement cannot cure."

However Othello claims in the play that he is "not easily jealous". The implication is that it would never have entered his head to suspect Desdemona of infidelity but for Iago's plot. There is no doubt that Shakespeare intended this claim to be true. Othello's final speech, just before his suicide, is an objective statement for the audience as well as for the people on stage, of the tragedy. Othello's character is neither flawless nor a completely flawed one. Had he been flawless, Iago would certainly not have succeeded in his designs? But nor are his claims for nobility hollow. The testimony of all the main characters in the play is decisive, Brabantio loved him; Lodovico speaks of him as 'the noble Moor', 'once so good'; Cassio, who has good cause to hate him, addresses him as 'Dear General' and speaks his epitaph: 'he was great of heart'. The Duke declares that he is more fair than black. Montano is delighted to hear of Othello's appointment as Governor.

Even Iago confesses that the state "Cannot with safety cast him" because "Another of his fathom they have none". When he first outlines his plot he declares in Act I; Scene (iii), lines 393-94:

> "The Moor is of a free and open nature,
> That thinks men honest that but seem to be so
> ...."

In a later soliloquy, he is even more emphatic (Act II; Scene 1, lines 279-80):

> The Moor—howbeit that I endure him not—
> Is of a constant, loving, noble nature...

Shakespeare also does not create the impression that Othello is given over to self-dramatization. His quiet authority when he encounters Brabantio's servants (Act I; Scene 2, line 59); his defence of his marriage before the senate and the last speech which leads to his account of stabbing the 'malignant and...turbaned Turk' as a preparation for his own suicide, are examples of his sense of occasion, which is perfectly fitting in a great soldier of royal birth. Even his frequent expressions of self-esteem would be regarded as legitimate and proper pride by Shakespeare's audience. Othello was perfectly justified in believing that his services to the state would out-tongue the complaints of Brabantio; he was right in believing that his royal birth and his merits made him worthy of Desdemona; and as he put it in his final apologia in Act V; Scene (ii) at line No. 335:

> "I have done the state some service and they
> know't"

Far from being a self-dramatizer, Othello is to be taken as modest in his claims, especially we keep in mind that in the Elizabethan context, it was believed that a great man need not necessarily be unconscious of his merits.

Another dimension of Othello's character is his supposed inability to recognize the extent of his own guilt. Some critics believe that Othello is to be seen blaming the arts of the demi-devil, Iago and fate rather than owning up his lack of judgement. A close study of the last scene would reveal the incompatibility of the text with this view. Immediately after the murder, even as Othello continues to believe in Desdemona's guilt, he is categorical in his regrets:

I have no wife
O, insupportable! O heavy hour!
Methinks it should be now a huge eclipse
Of sun and moon, and that th'affrighted globe
Should yawn at alteration.

(lines 98-102)

He later offers another explanation:

"It is the very error of the moon;
She comes more nearer earth than
she was wont,
And makes men mad"

Othello here is suggesting that he had been driven mad. But when Emilia seems to be shielding him by making out that Desdemona has committed suicide, Othello does face up to the brutal reality. He shows how terribly his reason had been clouded. Here is perhaps the dawning of the truth, as he exclaims at line No. 130,

"She's like a liar gone to burning hell"

Then comes his confession:

"O, I were damned beneath all depth in hell
But that I did proceed upon just grounds."

Even the defence that his grounds were just is taken away from Othello as he learns the truth. He now asks: 'Why should honour outlive honesty?' and intends to kill himself. He realizes that he has reached his journey's end.

It is only the evil characters in Shakespeare, like Edmund in *King Lear*, who completely discount the influence of the stars. Othello never disclaims his responsibility for his actions. He does ask "Who can control his fate?" and speaks of Desdemona as ill-starred. But he should be seen referring to the derivation of her name from a word which means 'unfortunate'. Othello does not deceive himself. He recognizes that he is damned and therefore he looks forward to an eternity of torture for his crime. Lines 271 to 278 contain the agony of his soul:

"When we shall meet and compt
This look of thine will hurl my soul from heaven
And fiends will snatch at it...
Whip me ye devils,
From the possession of this heavenly sight!
Blow me about in winds! Roast me in sulphur!
Wash me in steep-down gulfs of liquid fire!"

It would obviously be wrong to contend, even after reading these lines, that Othello refuses to recognize his own guilt. In his final speech, after reiterating the enormity of his deed, he stabs himself.

That Othello proves himself so credulous as to be easily mislead by Iago is to be seen in the context of the fact that Othello is comparatively ignorant of his wife. Shakespeare deliberately arranges the story in such a manner that Othello is given no time to live at all with his wife. The consummation of his marriage has to be postponed by the exigencies of the times and the first night in Cyprus is disturbed by the brawl which leads to Cassio's dismissal for drunken conduct. The next day Iago sets in motion his intrigue and he succeeds not because Othello is a simpleton but because he is ignorant of his wife's nature. As a matter of fact, Othello's experience of the world has been so one-sided that he can reasonably be taken to be unaware of the ways of the world. In Act I; Scene (iii) lines 86-87, he himself confesses:

"Little of this great world can I speak
More than pertains to feats of broil and battle..."

Together with this one-sidedness of his knowledge of the world goes the fact that even though he is a Christian, he retains his faith in some pagan superstitions. Just as he does not 'know' Desdemona, she, too, is unaware of his self in entirety. She has fallen in love with his autobiography—his account of himself—rather than with him. She "saw Othello's visage in his mind" and this made the difference of colour seem irrelevant. However the 'otherness' of Othello does not disappear just like that. Living together in harmony for at least some time would have led to that result but that was not to be. Difference in the respective ages of Othello and Desdemona further accentuates the temperamental differences between them. Othello has reached middle age, apparently without any previous experience of love, or to put it differently, without any knowledge of the manners and morals of Venetian ladies. In one respect, this affects Othello's knowledge of himself in relation to Desdemona. Equally important is his failure to know his capacity for jealousy—that, though he does not get "easily jealous", he could be wrought by spurious evidence and become affected greatly.

It is on account of his lack of experience of women and because he has no ostensible reason to suspect Iago's integrity or to know of his hidden hatred for himself, he comes to trust his comrade-in-arms instead of the bride, who is still somebody not fully known. However Othello's character in its human roundedness is perfectly credible. Dr. Johnson refers approvingly to "the fiery openness of Othello, magnanimous, artless, and credulous, boundless in his confidence, ardent in his affection, inflexible in his resolution and obdurate in his revenge." Iago only exploits the virtues as well as the weaknesses of the Moor and of Desdemona—weaknesses both of character and situation. The noble simplicity of Othello,

> Whose nature is so far from doing harm
> That he suspects none,

and the warmth of Desdemona in championing Cassio's cause are the two qualities which provide Iago with his opportunity; but he would not have succeeded without the defects in the two characters. Desdemona's advocacy of Cassio is an interference in professional matters. Desdemona overdoes it, almost to the point of nagging. Another blemish—serious in its effect even though one can understand why she felt inclined to do that—is the story she makes out about the handkerchief. May be she does so because she is shocked and frightened by Othello's outburst of fury.

Othello is certainly not blemishless. As has been seen earlier, his own transparent sincerity makes him absurdly credulous and ignorant of the devious intricacies of human nature. His simplistic sense of honour makes him believe that a man's honour can be blotted by his wife's misconduct and redeemed only by her death. He also has the delusion that his own conduct is most rational and that his own passions are in control. He errs grievously but later, after the murder, he learns how he had been deluded and what he had lost, he recovers his former nobility and his greatness of heart.

While pronouncing his own epitaph, Othello claims that he had "loved not wisely, but too well." One tends to accept as true. If he had loved less intensely, if he had not centered his very being on Desdemona, if she had not been the very source of life-giving inspiration for him, he certainly would have reacted differently to her supposed faithlessness. He retains some sympathy, even in his most abominable behaviour because we still remember his earlier nobility, reflected in the sheer poetry of his speeches, also perhaps because we are all the time conscious how he has become Iago's plaything, because we are aware of the struggle in his mind between love and his perverted views of 'honour' and also because he seems to be suffering from a profound spiritual disillusionment. Coleridge had this last factor in mind when he referred to "an agony that the creature, whom he had believed angelic...whom he could not help still loving, should be proved impure and worthless.... It was a moral indignation that virtue should so fall."

(vi) THE ROLE OF CHANCE IN THE PLAY

The conception of the play, the movement of it, the events in it, the bringing about of the catastrophe are all apparently in the realm of chance. Again and again a chance word from Desdemona, a chance meeting of Othello and Cassio, a question which anyone but Othello would have asked, would have destroyed Iago's plot and ended his life. In their stead, Fate steps in to help the villain in his game of revenge.

It is but chance that Iago could have been the only person who could have stooped to this level and it is only with the noble Moor that he could have behaved thus. The handkerchief is Fate's little irony. Desdemona's dropping it Emilia's picking it up, her passing it on to her husband, his lying to Othello about it and eventually Othello's bringing himself to the point of his oath—all form a chain which is based on Emilia's baffling silence. Emilia cannot confers to Desdemona perhaps because Iago and Cassio happen to come there. The coming of Cassio only when Iago has persuaded Othello to observe him (Cassio) rather than talk to him and the arrival of Bianca carrying the handkerchief are again fortuitous. Not only that. It is sheer chance that Cassio has escaped death at the hands of Roderigo since he was wearing his 'coat' by chance. It is again by chance that Emilia reaches Desdemona when life is ebbing out of Desdemona and Emilia thus exposes her husband's plot. The role of chance in the play cannot be ignored in any way.

THE TRAGEDY OF OTHELLO THE MOOR OF VENICE

THE ACTORS' NAME

OTHELLO, the Moor
BRABANTIO, Father to Desdemona
CASSIO, an Honourable Lieutenant
IAGO, a villain
RODERIGO, a gull'd Gentlemen
DUKE OF VENICE
SENATORS
MONTANO, Governor of Cyprus
GENTLEMEN OF CYPRUS
LODOVICO, and GRATIANO, two Noble Venetians
Sailors
Clown

DESDEMONA, wife of Othello
EMILIA, wife to Iago
BIANCA, a Courtesan

I.1

Enter Roderigo, and Iago

RODERIGO: Never tell me, I take it much unkindly
That thou (Iago) who hast had my purse,
As if the strings were thine, shouldst know of this.
IAGO: 'Sblood, but you'll not hear me. If ever I did dream
Of such a matter, abhor me.
RODERIGO: Thou told'st me,
Thou didst hold him in thy hate.
IAGO: Despise me
If I do not. Three Great-ones of the City
(In personal suit to make me his Lieutenant)
Off-capp'd to him: and by the faith of man
I know my price, I am worth no worse a place.
But he (as loving his own pride, and purposes)
Evades them, with a bumbast circumstance,
Horribly stuff'd with epithets of war,
And in conclusion,
Nonsuits my mediators. For certes, says he,
I have already chose my officer. And what was he?
Forsooth, a great arithmetician,
One Michael Cassio, a Florentine,
(A fellow almost damn'd in a fair wife)
That never set a squadron in the field,
Nor the division of a battle knows
More than a spinster. Unless the bookish theoric:
Wherein the toged Consuls can propose
As masterly as he. Mere prattle (without practice)
Is all his soldiership. But he (Sir) had th' election;

And I (of whom his eyes had seen the proof
At Rhodes, at Cyprus, and on other grounds,
Christen'd, and Heathen,) must be be-leed, and calm'd
By debitor, and creditor. This counter-caster,
He (in good time) must his Lieutenant be,
And I (God bless the mark) his Moorship's Ancient.
RODERIGO: By heaven, I rather would have been his hangman.
IAGO: Why, there's no remedy.
'Tis the curse of service;
Preferment goes by letter, and affection,
Not by old gradation, where each second
Stood heir to th' first. Now Sir, be judge yourself,
Whether I in any just term am affin'd
To love the Moor ?
RODERIGO: I would not follow him then.
IAGO: O Sir content you.
I follow him, to serve my turn upon him.
We cannot all be masters, nor all masters
Cannot be truly follow'd. You shall mark
Many a duteous and knee-crooking knave;
That (doting on his own obsequious bondage)
Wears out his time, much like his master's ass,
For nought but provender, and when he 's old cashier'd.
Whip me such honest knaves. Others there are
Who trimm'd in forms, and visages of duty,
Keep yet their hearts attending on themselves,
And throwing but shows of service on their Lords
Do well thrive by them.
And when they have lin'd their coats
Do themselves homage.
These fellows have some soul,
And such a one do I profess myself. For (Sir)
It is as sure as you are Roderigo,
Were I the Moor, I would not be Iago:
In following him, I follow but myself.
Heaven is my judge, not I for love and duty,

But seeming so, for my peculiar end:
For when my outward action doth demonstrate
The native act, and figure of my heart
In complement extern, 'tis not long after
But I will wear my heart upon my sleeve
For daws to peck at; I am not what I am.

RODERIGO: What a full fortune does the thick-lips owe
If he can carry 't thus?

IAGO: Call up her father:
Rouse him, make after him, poison his delight,
Proclaim him in the streets. Incense her kinsmen,
And though he in a fertile climate dwell,
Plague him with flies: though that his joy be joy,
Yet throw such chances of vexation on 't,
As it may lose some colour.

RODERIGO: Here is her father's house, I'll call aloud.

IAGO: Do, with like timorous accent, and dire yell,
As when (by night and negligence) the fire
Is spied in populous cities.

RODERIGO: What hoa: Brabantio, Signior Brabantio, hoa.

IAGO: Awake: what hoa, Brabantio: thieves, thieves.
Look to your house, your daughter, and your bags,
Thieves, thieves.

Enter Brabantio at a window.

BRABANTIO: What is the reason of this terrible summons?
What is the matter there?

RODERIGO: Signior is all your family within?

IAGO: Are your doors lock'd?

BRABANTIO: Why? Wherefore ask you this?

IAGO: Sir, y'are robb'd, for shame put on your gown,
Your heart is burst, you have lost half your soul;
Even now, now, very now, an old black ram
Is tupping your white ewe. Arise, arise,
Awake the snorting citizens with the bell,
Or else the devil will make a grandsire of you.
Arise I say.

BRABANTIO: What, have you lost your wits?
RODERIGO: Most reverend Signior, do you know my voice?
BRABANTIO: Not I: what are you?
RODERIGO: My name is Roderigo.
BRABANTIO: The worser welcome:
I have charg'd thee not to haunt about my doors:
In honest plainness thou hast heard me say,
My daughter is not for thee. And now in madness
(Being full of supper, and distemp'ring draughts)
Upon malicious knavery, dost thou come
To start my quiet.
RODERIGO: Sir, Sir, Sir.
BRABANTIO: But thou must needs be sure,
My spirits and my place have in their power
To make this bitter to thee.
RODERIGO: Patience good Sir.
BRABANTIO: What tell'st thou me of robbing?
This is Venice: my house is not a grange.
RODERIGO: Most grave Brabantio,
In simple and pure soul, I come to you.

IAGO: Sir: you are one of those that will not serve God, if the devil bid you. Because we come to do you service, and you think we are ruffians, you'll have your daughter cover'd with a Barbary horse, you'll have your nephews neigh to you, you'll have coursers for cousins: and gennets for germans.

BRABANTIO: What profane wretch art thou?

IAGO: I am one, Sir, that come to tell you, your daughter and the Moor, are making the beast with two backs.

BRABANTIO: Thou art a villain.

IAGO: You are a Senator.

BRABANTIO: This thou shalt answer. I know thee Roderigo.

RODERIGO : Sir, I will answer any thing. But I beseech you
If 't be your pleasure, and most wise consent,

(As partly I find it is) that your fair daughter,
At this odd even and dull watch o' th' night
Transported with no worse nor better guard,
But with a knave of common hire, a gondolier,
To the gross clasps of a lascivious Moor:
If this be known to you, and your allowance,
We then have done you bold, and saucy wrongs.
But if you know not this, my manners tell me,
We have your wrong rebuke. Do not believe
That from the sense of all civility,
I thus would play and trifle with your reverence.
Your daughter (if you have not given her leave)
I say again, hath made a gross revolt,
Tying her duty, beauty, wit, and fortunes
In an extravagant, and wheeling stranger,
Of here, and every where: straight satisfy yourself.
If she be in her chamber, or your house,
Let loose on me the justice of the State
For thus deluding you.

BRABANTIO: Strike on the tinder, hoa:
Give me a taper: call up all my people,
This accident is not unlike my dream,
Belief of it oppresses me already.
Light, I say, light. *Exit.*

IAGO: Farewell: for I must leave you.
It seems not meet, nor wholesome to my place
To be producted (as if I stay, I shall)
Against the Moor. For I do know the State,
(However this may gall him with some check)
Cannot with safety cast him. For he 's embark'd
With such loud reason to the Cyprus Wars,
(Which even now stands in act) that for their souls
Another of his fadom, they have none,
To lead their business. In which regard,
Though I do hate him as I do hell pains,
Yet, for necessity of present life,

I must show out a flag, and sign of love,
(Which is indeed but sign) that you shall surely find him:
Lead to the Sagittary, the raised search:
And there will I be with him. So farewell.

Exit.

Enter Brabantio, in his night-gown, and Servants with torches.

BRABANTIO: It is too true an evil. Gone she is,
And what 's to come of my despised time,
Is nought but bitterness. Now Roderigo,
Where didst thou see her? (Oh unhappy girl)
With the Moor say'st thou? (Who would be a father)
How didst thou know 'twas she? (Oh she deceives me
Past thought): what said she to you? Get moe tapers:
Raise all my kindred. Are they married think you?

RODERIGO: Truly I think they are.

BRABANTIO: Oh Heaven: how got she out?
Oh treason of the blood.
Fathers, from hence trust not your daughters' minds
By what you see them act. Is there not charms,
By which the property of youth, and maidhood
May be abus'd? Have you not read Roderigo,
Of some such thing?

RODERIGO: Yes sir: I have indeed.

BRABANTIO: Call up my brother: oh would you had had her.
Some one way, some another. Do you know
Where we may apprehend her, and the Moor?

RODERIGO: I think I can discover him, if you please
To get good guard, and go along with me.

BRABANTIO: Pray you lead on. At every house I'll call,
(I may command at most): get weapons (hoa)
And raise some special officers of might:
On good Roderigo, I will deserve your pains.

Exeunt.

I.2

Enter Othello, Iago, Attendants, with torches.

IAGO: Though in the trade of war I have slain men,
Yet do I hold it very stuff o' th' conscience
To do no contriv'd murder: I lack iniquity
Sometime to do me service. Nine, or ten times
I had thought t' have yerk'd him here under the ribs.
OTHELLO: 'Tis better as it is.
IAGO: Nay but he prated,
And spoke such scurvy, and provoking terms
Against your Honour, that with the little godliness I have
I did full hard forbear him. But I pray you Sir,
Are you fast married? Be assur'd of this,
That the Magnifico is much belov'd,
And hath in his effect a voice potential
As double as the Duke's: He will divorce you,
Or put upon you, what restraint or grievance,
The Law (with all his might, to enforce it on)
Will give him cable.
OTHELLO: Let him do his spite;
My services, which I have done the Signiory
Shall out-tongue his complaints. 'Tis yet to know,
Which when I know, that boasting is an honour,
I shall promulgate. I fetch my life and being,
From men of royal siege. And my demerits
May speak (unbonneted) to as proud a fortune
As this that I have reach'd. For know Iago,
But that I love the gentle Desdemona,
I would not my unhoused free condition
Put into circumscription, and confine,
For the sea's worth. But look, what lights come yond?

Enter Cassio, with torches.

IAGO: Those are the raised father, and his friends:
You were best go in.
OTHELLO: Not I: I must be found.
My parts, my title, and my perfect soul
Shall manifest me rightly. Is it they?
IAGO: By Janus, I think no.
OTHELLO: The servants of the Duke's?
And my Lieutenant?
The goodness of the night upon you (friends)
What is the news?
CASSIO: The Duke does greet you (General)
And he requires your haste, post-haste appearance,
Even on the instant.
OTHELLO: What is the matter, think you?
CASSIO: Something from Cyprus, as I may divine:
It is a business of some heat. The galleys
Have sent a dozen sequent messengers
This very night, at one another's heels:
And many of the Consuls, rais'd and met,
Are at the Duke's already. You have been hotly call'd for,
When being not at your lodging to be found,
The Senate hath sent about three several quests,
To search you out.
OTHELLO: 'Tis well I am found by you:
I will but spend a word here in the house,
And go with you.
CASSIO: Ancient, what makes he here?
IAGO: Faith, he tonight hath boarded a land carrack,
If it prove lawful prize, he's made for ever.
CASSIO: I do not understand.
IAGO: He 's married.
CASSIO: To who?
IAGO: Marry to – Come Captain, will you go?
OTHELLO: Have with you.
CASSIO: Here comes another troop to seek for you.

Enter Brabantio, Roderigo, with officers, and torches.

IAGO: It is Brabantio: General be advis'd,
He comes to bad intent.

OTHELLO: Holla, stand there.

RODERIGO: Signior, it is the Moor.

BRABANTIO: Down with him, thief,

IAGO: You, Roderigo? Come sir, I am for you.

OTHELLO: Keep up your bright swords, for the dew will rust them.
Good Signior, you shall more command with years,
Than with your weapons.

BRABANTIO: Oh thou foul thief,
Where hast thou stow'd my daughter?
Damn'd as thou art, thou hast enchanted her
For I'll refer me to all things of sense,
(If she in chains of magic were not bound)
Whether a maid, so tender, fair, and happy,
So opposite to marriage, that she shunn'd
The wealthy curled darling of our Nation,
Would ever have (t' incur a general mock)
Run from her guardage to the sooty bosom,
Of such a thing as thou: to fear, not to delight?
Judge me the world, if 'tis not gross in sense,
That thou hast practis'd on her with foul charms,
Abus'd her delicate youth, with drugs or minerals,
That weakens motion. I'll have 't disputed on,
'Tis probable, and palpable to thinking;
I therefore apprehend and do attach thee,
For an abuser of the World, a practiser
Of arts inhibited, and out of warrant;
Lay hold upon him, if he do resist
Subdue him, at his peril.

OTHELLO: Hold your hands
Both you of my inclining, and the rest.
Were it my cue to fight, I should have known it
Without a prompter. Whither will you that I go

To answer this your charge?
BRABANTIO: To prison, till fit time
Of Law, and course of direct Session
Call thee to answer.
OTHELLO: What if I do obey?
How may the Duke be therewith satisfi'd,
Whose messengers are here about my side,
Upon some present business of the State,
To bring me to him.
OFFICER: 'Tis true most worthy Signior,
The Duke 's in Council, and your noble self,
I am sure is sent for.
BRABANTIO: How? The Duke in Council?
In this time of the night? Bring him away:
Mine's not an idle cause. The Duke himself,
Or any of my brothers of the State,
Cannot but feel this wrong, as 'twere their own:
For if such actions may have passage free,
Bond-slaves, and pagans shall our Statesmen be.
Exeunt.

I.3

The Duke and Senators set at a table with lights and Attendants.

DUKE: There is no composition in this news,
That gives them credit.
1 SENATOR: Indeed, they are disproportioned;
My letters say, a hundred and seven galleys.
DUKE: And mine a hundred and forty.
2 SENATOR: And mine two hundred:
But though they jump not on a just accompt,

(As in these cases where the aim reports,
'Tis oft with difference) yet do they all confirm
A Turkish fleet, and bearing up to Cyprus.
DUKE: Nay, it is possible enough to judgement:
I do not so secure me in the error,
But the main article I do approve
In fearful sense.
SAILOR *within:* What hoa, what hoa, what hoa.

Enter Sailor.

OFFICER: A messenger from the galleys.
DUKE: Now? What 's the business?
SAILOR: The Turkish preparation makes for Rhodes,
So was I bid report here to the State,
By Signior Angelo.
DUKE: How say you by this change?
1 SENATOR: This cannot be
By no assay of reason. 'Tis a pageant
To keep us in false gaze, when we consider
Th' importancy of Cyprus to the Turk;
And let ourselves again but understand,
That as it more concerns the Turk than Rhodes,
So may he with more facile question bear it,
For that it stands not in such warlike brace,
But altogether lacks th' abilities
That Rhodes is dress'd in. If we make thought of this,
We must not think the Turk is so unskilful,
To leave that latest, which concerns him first,
Neglecting an attempt of ease, and gain
To wake, and wage a danger profitless.
DUKE: Nay, in all confidence he 's not for Rhodes.
OFFICER: Here is more news.

Enter a Messenger.

MESSENGER: The Ottomites, reverend, and gracious,
Steering with due course toward the Isle of Rhodes,
Have there injointed them with an after fleet.
1 SENATOR: Ay, so I thought: how many, as you guess?

MESSENGER: Of thirty sail: and now they do re-stem
Their backward course, bearing with frank appearance
Their purposes towards Cyprus. Signior Montano,
Your trusty and most valiant servitor,
With his free duty, recommends you thus,
And prays you to believe him.
DUKE: 'Tis certain then for Cyprus:
Marcus Luccicos is not he in town?
1 SENATOR: He 's now in Florence.
DUKE: Write from us,
To him post, post-haste, dispatch.
1 SENATOR: Here comes Brabantio, and the valiant Moor.

Enter Brabantio, Othello, Cassio, Iago, Roderigo, and Officers.

DUKE: Valiant Othello, we must straight employ you,
Against the general enemy Ottoman.
I did not see you: welcome gentle Signior,
We lack'd your counsel, and your help tonight.
BRABANTIO: So did I yours: Good your Grace pardon me.
Neither my place, nor aught I heard of business
Hath rais'd me from my bed; nor doth the general care
Take hold on me. For my particular grief
Is of so flood-gate, and o'erbearing nature,
That it engluts, and swallows other sorrows,
And it is still itself.
DUKE: Why? What 's the matter?
BRABANTIO: My daughter: oh my daughter!
SENATORS: Dead?
BRABANTIO: Ay, to me.
She is abus'd, stol'n from me, and corrupted
By spells, and medicines, bought of mountebanks;
For Nature, so prepost'rously to err,
(Being not deficient, blind, or lame of sense,)
Sans witchcraft could not.
DUKE: Whoe'er he be, that in this foul proceeding
Hath thus beguil'd your daughter of herself,

And you of her; the bloody Book of Law,
You shall yourself read, in the bitter letter,
After your own sense: yea, though our proper son
Stood in your action.
BRABANTIO: Humbly I thank your Grace,
Here is the man; this Moor, whom now it seems
Your special mandate, for the state affairs
Hath hither brought.
ALL: We are very sorry for 't.
DUKE: What in your own part, can you say to this?
BRABANTIO: Nothing, but this is so.
OTHELLO: Most potent, grave, and reverend Signiors,
My very noble, and approv'd good masters;
That I have ta'en away this old man's daughter,
It is most true: true I have married her;
The very head, and front of my offending,
Hath this extent; no more. Rude am I, in my speech.
And little blest with the soft phrase of peace;
For since these arms of mine, had seven years' pith,
Till now, some nine moons wasted, they have us'd
Their dearest action, in the tented field:
And little of this great world can I speak,
More than pertains to feats of broils, and battle,
And therefore little shall I grace my cause,
In speaking for myself. Yet, (by your gracious patience)
I will a round unvarnish'd tale deliver,
Of my whole course of love.
What drugs, what charms,
What conjuration, and what mighty magic,
(For such proceeding am I charg'd withal)
I won his daughter.
BRABANTIO: A maiden, never bold:
Of spirit so still, and quiet, that her motion
Blush'd at herself, and she, in spite of nature,
Of years, of country, credit, every thing,
To fall in love, with what she fear'd to look on;

It is a judgement maim'd, and most imperfect,
That will confess Perfection so could err
Against all rules of Nature, and must be driven
To find out practices of cunning hell
Why this should be. I therefore vouch again,
That with some mixtures, powerful o'er the blood,
Or with some dram, (conjur'd to this effect),
He wrought upon her.

DUKE: To vouch this, is no proof,
Without more wider, and more overt test
Than these thin habits, and poor likelihoods
Of modern seeming, do prefer against him.

SENATOR: But Othello, speak,
Did you, by indirect, and forced courses
Subdue, and poison this young maid's affections?
Or came it by request, and such fair question
As soul to soul affordeth?

OTHELLO: I do beseech you,
Send for the Lady to the Sagittary,
And let her speak of me before her father:
If you do find me foul, in her report,
The trust, the office, I do hold of you,
Not only take away, but let your sentence
Even fall upon my life.

DUKE: Fetch Desdemona hither.

Exit two or three.

OTHELLO: Ancient, conduct them:
You best know the place.

Exit Iago.

And till she come, as truly as to heaven,
I do confess the vices of my blood,
So justly to your grave ears, I'll present,
How I did thrive in this fair Lady's love,
And she in mine.

DUKE: Say it Othello.

OTHELLO: Her father lov'd me, oft invited me:

Still question'd me the story of my life,
From year to year: the battles, sieges, fortune,
That I have pass'd.
I ran it through, even from my boyish days,
To th' very moment that he bad me tell it.
Wherein I spoke of most disastrous chances:
Of moving accidents by flood and field,
Of hair-breadth 'scapes i' th' imminent deadly breach;
Of being taken by the insolent foe,
And sold to slavery. Of my redemption thence,
And portance in my traveller's history.
Wherein of antres vast, and deserts idle,
Rough quarries, rocks, hills, whose heads touch heaven,
It was my hint to speak. Such was my process,
And of the Cannibals that each other eat,
The Anthropophagi, and men whose heads
Do grow beneath their shoulders. These things to hear,
Would Desdemona seriously incline:
But still the house affairs would draw her hence:
Which ever as she could with haste dispatch,
She 'ld come again, and with a greedy ear
Devour up my discourse. Which I observing,
Took once a pliant hour, and found good means
To draw from her a prayer of earnest heart,
That I would all my pilgrimage dilate,
Whereof by parcels she had something heard,
But not intentively: I did consent,
And often did beguile her of her tears,
When I did speak of some distressful stroke
That my youth suffer'd: My story being done,
She gave me for my pains a world of sighs;
She swore in faith 'twas strange: 'twas passing strange,
'Twas pitiful: 'twas wondrous pitiful.
She wish'd she had not heard it, yet she wish'd
That Heaven had made her such a man. She thank'd me,
And bad me, if I had a friend that lov'd her,

I should but teach him how to tell my story,
And that would woo her. Upon this hint I spake,
She lov'd me for the dangers I had pass'd,
And I lov'd her, that she did pity them.
This only is the witchcraft I have us'd.
Here comes the Lady: Let her witness it.

Enter Desdemona, Iago, Attendants.

DUKE: I think this tale would win my daughter too,
Good Brabantio, take up this mangled matter at the best:
Men do their broken weapons rather use,
Than their bare hands.

BRABANTIO: I pray you hear her speak.
If she confess that she was half the wooer,
Destruction on my head, if my bad blame
Light on the man. Come hither gentle Mistress,
Do you perceive in all this noble company,
Where most you owe obedience?

DESDEMONA: My noble father,
I do perceive here a divided duty.
To you I am bound for life, and education:
My life and education both do learn me,
How to respect you. You are the Lord of duty,
I am hitherto your daughter. But here 's my husband;
And so much duty, as my mother show'd
To you, preferring you before her father:
So much I challenge, that I may profess
Due to the Moor my Lord.

BRABANTIO: God be with you: I have done.
Please it your Grace, on to the state affairs;
I had rather to adopt a child, than get it.
Come hither Moor;
I here do give thee that with all my heart,
Which but thou hast already, with all my heart
I would keep from thee. For your sake (Jewel)
I am glad at soul, I have no other child,
For thy escape would teach me tyranny

To hang clogs on them. I have done my Lord.
DUKE: Let me speak like yourself:
And lay a sentence,
Which as a grise, or step may help these lovers.
When remedies are past, the griefs are ended
By seeing the worst, which late on hopes depended.
To mourn a mischief that is past and gone,
Is the next way to draw new mischief on.
What cannot be preserv'd, when Fortune takes:
Patience, her injury a mock'ry makes.
The robb'd that smiles, steals something from the thief,
He robs himself, that spends a bootless grief.
BRABANTIO: So let the Turk of Cyprus us beguile,
We lose it not so long as we can smile:
He bears the sentence well, that nothing bears,
But the free comfort which from thence he hears.
But he bears both the sentence, and the sorrow,
That to pay grief, must of poor Patience borrow.
These sentences, to sugar, or to gall,
Being strong on both sides, are equivocal.
But words are words, I never yet did hear
That the bruis'd heart was pierc'd through the ear.
I humbly beseech you proceed to th' affairs of State.

DUKE: The Turk with a most mighty preparation makes for Cyprus: Othello, the fortitude of the place is best known to you. And though we have there a substitute of most allowed sufficiency; yet opinion, a more sovereign mistress of effects, throws a more safer voice on you: you must therefore be content to slubber the gloss of your new fortunes, with this more stubborn, and boist'rous expedition.

OTHELLO: The Tyrant Custom, most grave Senators,
Hath made the flinty and steel couch of War
My thrice-driven bed of down. I do agnize
A natural and prompt alacrity,
I find in hardness: and do undertake
This present wars against the Ottomites.

Most humbly therefore bending to your State,
I crave fit disposition for my wife,
Due reference of place, and exhibition,
With such accommodation and besort
As levels with her breeding.

DUKE: Why, at her father's.

BRABANTIO: I will not have it so.

OTHELLO: Nor I.

DESDEMONA: Nor would I there reside,
To put my father in impatient thoughts
By being in his eye. Most gracious Duke,
To my unfolding, lend your prosperous ear,
And let me find a charter in your voice
T' assist my simpleness.

DUKE: What would you Desdemona?

DESDEMONA: That I did love the Moor, to live with him,
My downright violence, and storm of fortunes,
May trumpet to the world. My heart's subdu'd
Even to the very quality of my Lord;
I saw Othello's visage in his mind,
And to his honours and his valiant parts,
Did I my soul and fortunes consecrate.
So that (dear Lords) if I be left behind
A moth of peace, and he go to the war,
The rites for why I love him, are bereft me:
And I a heavy interim shall support
By his dear absence. Let me go with him.

OTHELLO: Let her have your voice.
Vouch with me Heaven, I therefore beg it not
To please the palate of my appetite:
Nor to comply with heat the young affects
In my defunct, and proper satisfaction.
But to be free, and bounteous to her mind:
And Heaven defend your good souls, that you think
I will your serious and great business scant
When she is with me. No, when light-wing'd toys

Of feather'd Cupid, seel with wanton dullness
My speculative, and offic'd instrument:
That my disports corrupt, and taint my business:
Let housewives make a skillet of my helm,
And all indign, and base adversities,
Make head against my estimation.
DUKE: Be it as you shall privately determine,
Either for her stay, or going: th' affair cries haste:
And speed must answer it.
SENATOR: You must away tonight,
OTHELLO: With all my heart.
DUKE: At nine i' th' morning, here we'll meet again.
Othello, leave some officer behind
And he shall our commission bring to you:
And such things else of quality and respect
As doth import you.
OTHELLO: So please your Grace, my Ancient,
A man he is of honesty and trust:
To his conveyance I assign my wife,
With what else needful, your good Grace shall think
To be sent after me.
DUKE: Let it be so:
Good night to every one. And noble Signior,
If virtue no delighted beauty lack,
Your son-in-law is far more fair than black.
SENATOR: Adieu brave Moor, use Desdemona well.
BRABANTIO: Look to her (Moor) if thou hast eyes to see:
She has deceiv'd her father, and may thee.
Exeunt Duke, Senators, Officers, &c.
OTHELLO: My life upon her faith. Honest Iago,
My Desdemona must I leave to thee:
I prithee let thy wife attend on her,
And bring them after in the best advantage.
Come Desdemona, I have but an hour
Of love, of wordly matter, and direction
To spend with thee. We must obey the time.

Exeunt Othello and Desdemona.

RODERIGO: Iago.

IAGO: What say'st thou noble heart?

RODERIGO: What will I do, think'st thou?

IAGO: Why go to bed and sleep.

RODERIGO: I will incontinently drown myself.

IAGO: If thou dost, I shall never love thee after. Why thou silly gentleman?

RODERIGO: It is silliness to live, when to live is torment: and then have we a prescription to die, when death is our physician.

IAGO: Oh villainous: I have look'd upon the world for four times seven years, and since I could distinguish betwixt a benefit, and an injury: I never found man that knew how to love himself. Ere I would say, I would drown myself for the love of a guinea hen, I would change my humanity with a baboon.

RODERIGO: What should I do? I confess it is my shame to be so fond, but it is not in my virtue to amend it.

IAGO: Virtue? A fig, 'tis in ourselves that we are thus, or thus. Our bodies are our gardens, to the which, our wills are gardeners. So that if we will plant nettles, or sow lettuce: Set hyssop, and weed up thyme: Supply it with one gender of herbs, or distract it with many: either to have it sterile with idleness, or manur'd with industry, why the power, and corrigible authority of this lies in our wills. If the brain of our lives had not one scale of reason, to poise another of sensuality, the blood, and baseness of our natures would conduct us to most prepost'rous conclusions. But we have reason to cool our raging motions, our carnal stings, or unbitted lusts: whereof I take this, that you call love, to be a sect, or scion.

RODERIGO: It cannot be.

IAGO: It is merely a lust of the blood, and a permission of the will. Come, be a man: drown thyself? Drown cats, and blind puppies. I have profess'd me thy friend, and I confess me knit to thy deserving, with cables of perdurable toughness. I could never better stead thee than now. Put money in thy purse: follow thou the wars, defeat thy favour, with an usurp'd beard. I say put money in thy purse. It cannot be long that Desdemona should continue her love to the Moor. Put money in thy purse: nor he his to her. It was a violent commencement in her, and thou shalt see an answerable sequestration, put but money in thy purse. These Moors are changeable in their wills: fill thy purse with money. The food that to him now is as luscious as locusts, shall be to him shortly, as bitter as coloquintida. She must change for youth: when she is sated with his body she will find the errors of her choice. Therefore, put money in thy purse. If thou wilt needs damn thyself, do it a more delicate way than drowning. Make all the money thou canst: If sanctimony, and a frail vow, betwixt an erring barbarian, and super-subtle Venetian be not too hard for my wits, and all the tribe of hell, thou shalt enjoy her: therefore make money: a pox of drowning thyself, it is clean out of the way. Seek thou rather to be hang'd in compassing thy joy, than to be drown'd, and go without her.

RODERIGO: Wilt thou be fast to my hopes, if I depend on the issue?

IAGO: Thou art sure of me: go make money: I have told thee often, and I retell thee again, and again, I hate the Moor. My cause is hearted; thine hath no less reason. Let us be conjunctive in our revenge, against him. If thou canst cuckold him, thou dost thyself a pleasure, and me a sport. There are many events in the womb of Time, which will be delivered. Traverse, go, provide thy money. We will have more of this tomorrow. Adieu.

RODERIGO: Where shall we meet i' th' morning?

IAGO: At my lodging.

RODERIGO: I'll be with thee betimes.

IAGO: Go to, farewell. Do you hear Roderigo?

RODERIGO: I'll sell all my land.

Exit.

IAGO: Thus do I ever make my fool, my purse:
For I mine own gain'd knowledge should profane

If I would time expend with such a snipe,
But for my sport, and profit: I hate the Moor,
And it is thought abroad, that 'twixt my sheets
He 's done my office. I know not if 't be true,
But I, for mere suspicion in that kind,
Will do, as if for surety. He holds me well,
The better shall my purpose work on him:
Cassio 's a proper man: Let me see now,
To get his place, and to plume up my will
In double knavery. How? How? Let 's see.
After some time, to abuse Othello's ears,
That he is too familiar with his wife:
He hath a person, and a smooth dispose
To be suspected: fram'd to make women false.
The Moor is of a free, and open nature,
That thinks men honest, that but seem to be so,
And will as tenderly be led by th' nose
As asses are:
I have 't: it is engender'd: Hell, and Night,
Must bring this monstrous birth, to the world's light.

Exit.

II.1

Enter Montano, Governor of Cyprus, and two Gentlemen.

MONTANO: What from the Cape, can you discern at sea?
1 GENTLEMAN: Nothing at all, it is a high wrought flood:
I cannot 'twixt the heaven, and the main,
Descry a sail.
MONTANO: Methinks, the wind hath spoke aloud at land,
A fuller blast ne'er shook our battlements:
If it hath ruffian'd so upon the sea,

What ribs of oak, when the mountains melt on them,
Can hold the mortise. What shall we hear of this?

2 GENTLEMAN: A segregation of the Turkish Fleet:
For do but stand upon the foaming shore,
The chidden billow seems to pelt the clouds,
The wind-shak'd surge, with high and monstrous main
Seems to cast water on the burning Bear,
And quench the guards of th' ever-fixed Pole:
I never did like molestation view
On the enchafed flood.

MONTANO: If that the Turkish Fleet
Be not enshelter'd, and embay'd, they are drown'd,
It is impossible to bear it out.

Enter a Gentleman.

3 GENTLEMAN: News Lads: our wars are done:
The desperate tempest hath so bang'd the Turks,
That their designment halts. A noble ship of Venice,
Hath seen a grievous wrack and sufferance
On most part of their fleet.

MONTANO: How? Is this true?

3 GENTLEMAN: The ship is here put in: a Veronesa, Michael Cassio
Lieutenant to the warlike Moor, Othello,
Is come on shore: the Moor himself at sea,
And is in full commission here for Cyprus.

MONTANO: I am glad on 't:
'Tis a worthy Governor.

3 GENTLEMAN: But this same Cassio, though he speak of comfort,
Touching the Turkish loss, yet he looks sadly,
And prays the Moor be safe; for they were parted
With foul and violent tempest.

MONTANO: Pray Heavens he be:
For I have serv'd him, and the man commands
Like a full soldier. Let 's to the seaside (hoa)
As well to see the vessel that 's come in,

As to throw out our eyes for brave Othello,
Even till we make the main, and th' aerial blue,
An indistinct regard.

3 GENTLEMAN: Come, let 's do so;
For every minute is expectancy
Of more arrivance.

Enter Cassio.

CASSIO: Thanks, you the valiant of the warlike Isle,
That so approve the Moor: Oh let the Heavens
Give him defence against the elements,
For I have lost him on a dangerous sea.

MONTANO: Is he well shipp'd?

CASSIO: His bark is stoutly timber'd, and his pilot
Of very expert, and approv'd allowance;
Therefore my hopes (not surfeited to death)
Stand in bold cure.

WITHIN: A sail, a sail, a sail.

CASSIO: What noise?

2 GENTLEMAN: The Town is empty; on the brow o' th' sea
Stand ranks of people, and they cry, a sail.

CASSIO: My hopes do shape him for the Governor. *A shot.*

2 GENTLEMAN: They do discharge their shot of courtesy, Our friends, at least.

CASSIO: I pray you Sir, go forth,
And give us truth who 'tis that is arriv'd.

2 GENTLEMAN: I shall. *Exit.*

MONTANO: But good Lieutenant, is your General wiv'd?

CASSIO: Most fortunately: he hath achiev'd a Maid
That paragons description, and wild fame:
One that excels the quirks of blazoning pens,
And in th' essential vesture of creation,
Does tire the ingeniver.

Enter Gentleman.

How now? Who has put in?

2 GENTLEMAN: 'Tis one Iago, Ancient to the General.

CASSIO: Ha's had most favourable, and happy speed:

Tempests themselves, high seas, and howling winds,
The gutter'd rocks, and congregated sands,
Traitors ensteep'd, to enclog the guiltless keel,
As having sense of beauty, do omit
Their mortal natures, letting go safely by
The divine Desdemona.

MONTANO: What is she?

CASSIO: She that I spake of:
Our great Captain's Captain,
Left in the conduct of the bold Iago,
Whose footing here anticipates our thoughts,
A sennight's speed. Great Jove, Othello guard,
And swell his sail with thine own powerful breath,
That he may bless this Bay with his tall ship,
Make love's quick pants in Desdemona's arms,
Give renew'd fire to our extincted spirits.

Enter Desdemona, Iago, Roderigo, and Emilia.

Oh behold,
The riches of the ship is come on shore:
You men of Cyprus, let her have your knees.
Hail to thee Lady: and the grace of Heaven,
Before, behind thee, and on every hand
Enwheel thee round.

DESDEMONA: I thank you, valiant Cassio,
What tidings can you tell me of my Lord?

CASSIO: He is not yet arriv'd, nor know I aught
But that he 's well, and will be shortly here.

DESDEMONA: Oh, but I fear:
How lost you company?

CASSIO: The great contention of sea, and skies
Parted our fellowship. But hark, a sail.

WITHIN: A sail, a sail.

2 GENTLEMAN: They give this greeting to the Citadel:
This likewise is a friend.

CASSIO: See for the news:
Good Ancient, you are welcome. Welcome Mistress:

Let it not gall your patience (good Iago)
That I extend my manners. 'Tis my breeding,
That gives me this bold show of courtesy.

IAGO: Sir, would she give you so much of her lips,
As of her tongue she oft bestows on me,
You would have enough.

DESDEMONA: Alas: she has no speech.

IAGO: In faith too much:
I find it still, when I have leave to sleep.
Many before your Ladyship, I grant,
She puts her tongue a little in her heart,
And chides with thinking.

EMILIA: You have little cause to say so.

IAGO: Come on, come on: you are pictures out of door: bells in your parlours: wild-cats in your kitchens: saints in your injuries: devils being offended: players in your housewifery, and housewives in your beds.

DESDEMONA: Oh, fie upon thee, slanderer.

IAGO: Nay, it is true: or else I am a Turk,
You rise to play, and go to bed to work.

EMILIA: You shall not write my praise.

IAGO: No, let me not.

DESDEMONA: What wouldst write of me, if thou shouldst praise me?

IAGO: Oh, gentle Lady, do not put me to 't,
For I am nothing, if not critical.

DESDEMONA: Come on, assay.
There 's one gone to the Harbour?

IAGO: Ay Madam.

DESDEMONA: I am not merry: but I do beguile
The thing I am, by seeming otherwise.
Come, how wouldst thou praise me?

IAGO: I am about it, but indeed my invention comes from my pate, as birdlime does from freeze, it plucks out brains and all. But my Muse labours, and thus she is deliver'd.

If she be fair, and wise: fairness, and wit,
The one 's for use, the other useth it.

DESDEMONA: Well prais'd:
How if she be black and witty?

IAGO: *If she be black, and thereto have a wit,*
She'll find a white, that shall her blackness fit.

DESDEMONA: Worse, and worse.

EMILIA: How if fair and foolish?

IAGO: *She never yet was foolish that was fair,*
For even her folly help'd her to an heir.

DESDEMONA: These are old fond paradoxes, to make fools laugh i' th' alehouse. What miserable praise hast thou for her that's foul, and foolish.

IAGO: *There 's none so foul and foolish thereunto,*
But does foul pranks, which fair, and wise ones do.

DESDEMONA: Oh heavy ignorance: thou praisest the worst best. But what praise couldst thou bestow on a deserving woman indeed? One, that in the authority of her merit, did justly put on the vouch of very malice itself.

IAGO: *She that was ever fair, and never proud,*
Had tongue at will, and yet was never loud:
Never lack'd gold, and yet went never gay,
Fled from her wish, and yet said now I may.
She that being anger'd, her revenge being nigh,
Bad her wrong stay, and her displeasure fly:
She that in wisdom never was so frail,
To change the cod's head for the salmon's tail:
She that could think, and ne'er disclose her mind,
See suitors following, and not look behind:
She was a wight, (if ever such wights were)

DESDEMONA: To do what?

IAGO: To suckle fools, and chronicle small beer.

DESDEMONA: Oh most lame and impotent conclusion. Do not learn of him Emilia, though he be thy husband. How say you (Cassio) is he not a most profane, and liberal counsellor?

CASSIO: He speaks home (Madam) you may relish him more in the soldier, than in the scholar.

IAGO: He takes her by the palm: ay, well said, whisper. With as little a web as this, will I ensnare as great a fly as Cassio. Ay smile upon her, do: I will give thee in thine own courtship. You say true, 'tis so indeed. If such tricks as these strip you out of your lieutenantry, it had been better you had not kiss'd your three fingers so oft, which now again you are most apt to play the Sir, in. Very good: well kiss'd, and excellent courtesy: 'tis so indeed. Yet again, your fingers to your lips? Would they were clyster-pipes for your sake. [Trumpets within.] The Moor. I know his trumpet.

CASSIO: 'Tis truly so.

DESDEMONA: Let 's meet him, and receive him.

CASSIO: Lo, where he comes.

Enter Othello, and Attendants.

OTHELLO: O, my fair warrior.

DESDEMONA: My dear Othello.

OTHELLO: It gives me wonder, great as my content
To see you here before me.
Oh my soul's joy:
If after every tempest, come such calms,
May the winds blow, till they have waken'd death:
And let the labouring bark climb hills of seas
Olympus high: and duck again as low,
As hell 's from Heaven. If it were now to die,
'Twere now to be most happy. For I fear,
My soul hath her content so absolute,
That not another comfort like to this,
Succeeds in unknown fate.

DESDEMONA: The Heavens forbid
But that our loves
And comforts should increase
Even as our days do grow.

OTHELLO: Amen to that (sweet Powers)
I cannot speak enough of this content,
It stops me here: it is too much of joy.
And this, and this the greatest discords be *They kiss.*
That e'er our hearts shall make.

IAGO: Oh you are well tun'd now: But I'll set down the pegs that make this music, as honest as I am.

OTHELLO: Come: let us to the Castle.
News (Friends) our wars are done:
The Turks are drown'd.
How does my old acquaintance of this Isle?
(Honey) you shall be well desir'd in Cyprus,
I have found great love amongst them. Oh my Sweet,
I prattle out of fashion, and I dote
In mine own comforts. I prithee, good Iago,
Go to the Bay, and disembark my coffers:
Bring thou the Master to the Citadel,
He is a good one, and his worthiness
Does challenge much respect. Come, Desdemona,
Once more well met at Cyprus.

Exeunt Othello and Desdemona.

IAGO: Do thou meet me presently at the Harbour. Come thither, if thou be'st valiant, (as they say base men being in love, have then a nobility in their natures, more than is native to them) list me; the Lieutenant tonight watches on the Court of Guard. First, I must tell thee this: Desdemona, is directly in love with him.

RODERIGO: With him? Why, 'tis not possible.

IAGO: Lay thy finger thus: and let thy soul be instructed. Mark me with what violence she first lov'd the Moor, but for bragging, and telling her fantastical lies. To love him still for prating, let not thy discreet heart think it. Her eye must be fed. And what delight shall she have to look on the devil? When the blood is made dull with the act of sport, there should be a game to inflame it, and to give satiety a fresh appetite. Loveliness in favour, sympathy in years, manners, and beauties: all which the Moor is defective in. Now for want of these requir'd conveniences, her delicate tenderness will find itself abus'd, begin to heave the gorge, disrelish and abhor the Moor, very Nature will instruct her in it, and compel her to some second choice. Now Sir, this granted (as it is a most pregnant and unforc'd position) who stands so eminent in the degree of this fortune, as

Cassio does: a knave very voluble: no further conscionable, than in putting on the mere form of civil, and humane seeming, for the better compass of his salt, and most hidden loose affection? Why none, why none: A slipper, and subtle knave, a finder of occasion: that he's an eye can stamp, and counterfeit advantages, though true advantage never present itself. A devilish knave: besides, the knave is handsome, young: and hath all those requisites in him, that folly and green minds look after. A pestilent complete knave, and the woman hath found him already.

RODERIGO: I cannot believe that in her, she 's full of most bless'd condition.

IAGO: Bless'd fig's end. The wine she drinks is made of grapes. If she had been bless'd, she would never have lov'd the Moor: Bless'd pudding. Didst thou not see her paddle with the palm of his hand? Didst not mark that?

RODERIGO: Yes, that I did: but that was but courtesy.

IAGO: Lechery by this hand: an index, and obscure prologue to the history of lust and foul thoughts. They met so near with their lips, that their breaths embrac'd together. Villainous thoughts Roderigo, when these mutabilities so marshal the way, hard at hand comes the master, and main exercise, th' incorporate conclusion: Pish. But Sir, be you rul'd by me. I have brought you from Venice. Watch you tonight: for the command, I'll lay 't upon you. Cassio knows you not: I'll not be far from you. Do you find some occasion to anger Cassio, either by speaking too loud, or tainting his discipline, or from what other course you please, which the time shall more favourably minister.

RODERIGO: Well.

IAGO: Sir, he's rash, and very sudden in choler: and haply may strike at you, provoke him that he may: for even out of that will I cause these of Cyprus to mutiny. Whose qualification shall come into no true taste again, but by the displanting of Cassio. So shall you have a shorter journey to your desires, by the means I shall then have to prefer them. And the impediment most profitably removed, without the which there were no expectation of our prosperity.

RODERIGO: I will do this, if you can bring it to any opportunity.

IAGO: I warrant thee. Meet me by and by at the Citadel.
I must fetch his necessaries ashore. Farewell.

RODERIGO: Adieu. *Exit.*

IAGO: That Cassio loves her, I do well believe 't:
That she loves him, 'tis apt, and of great credit.
The Moor (howbeit that I endure him not)
Is of a constant, loving, noble nature,
And I dare think, he'll prove to Desdemona
A most dear-husband. Now I do love her too,
Not out of absolute lust, (though peradventure
I stand accomptant for as great a sin)
But partly led to diet my revenge,
For that I do suspect the lusty Moor
Hath leap'd into my seat. The thought whereof,
Doth (like a poisonous mineral) gnaw my inwards:
And nothing can, or shall content my soul
Till I am even'd with him, wife, for wife.
Or failing so, yet that I put the Moor,
At least into a jealousy so strong
That judgement cannot cure. Which thing to do,
If this poor Trash of Venice, whom I trace
For his quick hunting, stand the putting on,
I'll have our Michael Cassio on the hip,
Abuse him to the Moor, in the right garb
(For I fear Cassio with my night-cap too)
Make the Moor thank me, love me, and reward me,
For making him egregiously an ass,
And practising upon his peace, and quiet,
Even to madness. 'Tis here: but yet confus'd,
Knavery's plain face, is never seen, till us'd.

Exit.

II.2

Enter Othello's Herald with a proclamation.

HERALD: It is Othello's pleasure, our noble and valiant General. That upon certain tidings now arriv'd, importing the mere perdition of the Turkish Fleet: every man put himself into triumph. Some to dance, some to make bonfires, each man, to what sport and revels his addition leads him. For besides these beneficial news, it is the celebration of his nuptial. So much was his pleasure should be proclaimed. All offices are open, and there is full liberty of feasting from this present hour of five, till the bell hath told eleven. Heaven bless the Isle of Cyprus, and our noble General Othello.

Exit.

Enter Othello, Desdemona, Cassio, and Attendants.

OTHELLO: Good Michael, look you to the guard tonight.
Let's teach ouselves that honourable stop,
Not to out-sport discretion.

CASSIO: Iago hath direction what to do.
But notwithstanding with my personal eye
Will I look to 't.

OTHELLO: Iago is most honest:
Michael, good night. Tomorrow with your earliest,
Let me have speech with you. Come my dear Love,
The purchase made, the fruits are to ensue,
That profit 's yet to come 'tween me, and you.
Good night.

Exeunt Othello, Desdemona, and Attendants.

Enter Iago.

CASSIO: Welcome Iago: we must to the watch.

IAGO: Not this hour Lieutenant: 'tis not yet ten o' th' clock. Our General cast us thus early for the love of his

Desdemona: Who, let us not therefore blame; he hath not yet made wanton the night with her: and she is sport for Jove.

CASSIO: She 's a most exquisite Lady.

IAGO: And I'll warrant her, full of game.

CASSIO: Indeed she is a most fresh and delicate creature.

IAGO: What an eye she has?
Methinks it sounds a parley to provocation.

CASSIO: An inviting eye:
And yet methinks right modest.

IAGO: And when she speaks,
Is it not an alarum to Love?

CASSIO: She is indeed perfection.

IAGO: Well: happiness to their sheets. Come Lieutenant, I have a stoup of wine, and here without are a brace of Cyprus Gallants, that would fain have a measure to the health of black Othello.

CASSIO: Not tonight, good Iago, I have very poor, and unhappy brains for drinking. I could well wish courtesy would invent some other custom of entertainment.

IAGO: Oh, they are our friends: but one cup, I'll drink for you.

CASSIO: I have drunk but one cup tonight, and that was craftily qualified too: and behold what innovation it makes here. I am infortunate in the infirmity, and dare not task my weakness with any more.

IAGO: What man? 'Tis a night of revels, the Gallants desire it.

CASSIO: Where are they?

IAGO: Here, at the door: I pray you call them in.

CASSIO: I'll do 't, but it dislikes me. *Exit.*

IAGO: If I can fasten but one cup upon him
With that which he hath drunk tonight already,
He'll be as full of quarrel, and offence
As my young Mistress' dog.
Now my sick fool Roderigo,
Whom Love hath turn'd almost the wrong side out,
To Desdemona hath tonight carous'd,
Potations, pottle-deep; and he 's to watch.

Three else of Cyprus, noble swelling spirits,
(That hold their honours in a wary distance,
The very elements of this warlike Isle)
Have I tonight fluster'd with flowing cups,
And they watch too.
Now 'mongst this flock of drunkards
Am I to put our Cassio in some action
That may offend the Isle. But here they come.

Enter Cassio, Montano, and Gentlemen.

If consequence do but approve my dream,
My boat sails freely, both with wind and stream.

CASSIO: 'Fore God, they have given me a rouse already.

MONTANO: Good faith a little one: not past a pint, as I am a soldier.

IAGO: Some wine hoa.

And let me the canakin clink, clink:
And let me the canakin clink.
A soldier's a man: Oh, man's life 's but a span,
Why then let a soldier drink.

Some wine boys.

CASSIO: 'Fore God: an excellent song.

IAGO: I learn'd it in England: where indeed they are most potent in potting. Your Dane, your German, and your swag-belli'd Hollander (drink hoa) are nothing to your English.

CASSIO: Is your Englishmen so exquisite in his drinking?

IAGO: Why, he drinks you with facility, your Dane dead drunk. He sweats not to overthrow your Almain. He gives your Hollander a vomit, ere the next pottle can be fill'd.

CASSIO: To the health of our General.

MONTANO: I am for it Lieutenant: and I'll do you justice.

IAGO: Oh sweet England.

King Stephen was and a worthy peer,
His breeches cost him but a crown,
He held them sixpence all too dear,
With that he call'd the tailor town:
He was a wight of high renown,

And thou art but of low degree:
'Tis pride that pulls the country down,
Then take thy auld cloak about thee.

Some wine hoa.

CASSIO: 'Fore God, this is a more exquisite song than the other.

IAGO: Will you hear 't again?

CASSIO: No: for I hold him to be unworthy of his place, that does those things. Well: God's above all: and there be souls must be saved, and there be souls must not be saved.

IAGO: It is true, good Lieutenant.

CASSIO: For mine own part, no offence to the General, nor any man of quality: I hope to be saved.

IAGO: And so do I too Lieutenant.

CASSIO: Ay: (but by your leave) not before me. The Lieutenant is to be saved before the Ancient. Let 's have no more of this: let 's to our affairs. God forgive us our sins: Gentlemen let 's look to our business. Do not think Gentlemen, I am drunk: this is my Ancient, this is my right hand, and this is my left. I am not drunk now: I can stand well enough, and I speak well enough.

GENTLEMEN: Excellent well.

CASSIO: Why very well then: you must not think then, that I am drunk. Exit.

MONTANO: To th' platform (Masters) come, let 's set the watch.

IAGO: You see this fellow, that is gone before,
He is a soldier, fit to stand by Caesar,
And give direction. And do but see his vice,
'Tis to his virtue, a just equinox,
The one as long as th' other. 'Tis pity of him!
I fear the trust Othello puts him in,
On some odd time of his infirmity
Will shake this Island.

MONTANO: But is he often thus?

IAGO: 'Tis evermore his prologue to his sleep.
He'll watch the horologe a double set,

If drink rock not his cradle.

MONTANO: It were well
The General were put in mind of it:
Perhaps he sees it not, or his good nature
Prizes the virtue that appears in Cassio,
And looks not on his evils: is not this true?

Enter Roderigo.

IAGO: How now Roderigo?
I pray you after the Lieutenant, go.

Exit Roderigo.

MONTANO: And 'tis great pity, that the noble Moor
Should hazard such a place, as his own second
With one of an ingraft infirmity;
It were an honest action, to say so
To the Moor,

IAGO: Not I, for this fair Island,
I do love Cassio well: and would do much

Within: Help, help.

To cure him of his evil. But hark what noise?

Enter Cassio, pursuing Roderigo.

CASSIO: 'Zounds, you rogue: you rascal.

MONTANO: What 's the matter Lieutenant?

CASSIO: A knave teach me my duty? I'll beat the knave into a twiggen bottle.

RODERIGO: Beat me?

CASSIO: Dost thou prate, Rogue?

MONTANO: Nay, good Lieutenant:
I pray you Sir, hold your hand.

CASSIO: Let me go (Sir)
Or I'll knock you o'er the mazzard.

MONTANO: Come, come: you're drunk.

CASSIO: Drunk?

They fight.

IAGO: Away I say: go out and cry a mutiny.

Exit Roderigo. A bell rung.

Nay good Lieutenant. God's will Gentlemen:

Help hoa. Lieutenant. Sir Montano:
Help Masters. Here 's a goodly watch indeed.
Who 's that which rings the bell. Diablo, hoa:
The Town will rise. God's will Lieutenant,
You will be asham'd for ever.

Enter Othello, and Attendants with weapons.

OTHELLO: What is the matter here?
MONTANO: 'Zounds, I bleed still, I am hurt to th' death.
OTHELLO: Hold for your lives,
IAGO: Hold hoa. Lieutenant, Sir Montano, Gentlemen:
Have you forgot all sense of place and duty?
Hold. The General speaks to you: hold for shame.
OTHELLO: Why how now hoa? From whence ariseth this?
Are we turn'd Turks? and to ourselves do that
Which Heaven hath forbid the Ottomites.
For Christian shame, put by this barbarous brawl:
He that stirs next, to carve for his own rage,
Holds his soul light: He dies upon his motion.
Silence that dreadful bell, it frights the Isle,
From her propriety. What is the matter, Masters?
Honest Iago that looks dead with grieving,
Speak: who began this? On thy love I charge thee.
IAGO: I do not know: friends all, but now, even now.
In quarter, and in terms like bride, and groom
Devesting them for bed: and then, but now:
(As if some planet had unwitted men)
Swords out, and tilting one at other's breasts,
In opposition bloody. I cannot speak
Any beginning to this peevish odds.
And would, in action glorious, I had lost
Those legs, that brought me to a part of it.
OTHELLO: How comes it (Michael) you are thus forgot?
CASSIO: I pray you pardon me, I cannot speak.
OTHELLO: Worthy Montano, you were wont to be civil:
The gravity, and stillness of your youth
The world hath noted. And your name is great

In mouths of wisest censure. What 's the matter
That you unlace your reputation thus,
And spend your rich opinion, for the name
Of a night-brawler? Give me answer to it,

MONTANO: Worthy Othello, I am hurt to danger,
Your officer Iago, can inform you,
While I spare speech which something now offends me.
Of all that I do know, nor know I aught
By me, that 's said, or done amiss this night,
Unless self-charity be sometimes a vice,
And to defend ourselves, it be a sin
When violence assails us.

OTHELLO: Now by Heaven,
My blood begins my safer guides to rule,
And passion (having my best judgement collied)
Assays to lead the way. Zounds if I stir,
Or do but lift this arm, the best of you
Shall sink in my rebuke. Give me to know
How this foul rout began: Who set it on,
And he that is approv'd in this offence,
Though he had twinn'd with me, both at a birth,
Shall lose me. What in a town of war,
Yet wild, the people's hearts brim-full of fear,
To manage private, and domestic quarrel?
In night, and on the Court and Guard of safety?
'Tis monstrous: Iago, who began 't?

MONTANO: If partially affin'd, or leagu'd in office,
Thou dost deliver more, or less than truth,
Thou art no soldier.

IAGO: Touch me not so near,
I had rather have this tongue cut from my mouth,
Than it should do offence to Michael Cassio.
Yet I persuade myself, to speak the truth,
Shall nothing wrong him. This it is General:
Montano and myself being in speech,
There comes a fellow crying out for help,

And Cassio following him with determin'd sword
To execute upon him. Sir, this Gentleman,
Steps in to Cassio, and entreats his pause:
Myself, the crying fellow did pursue,
Lest by his clamour (as it so fell out)
The Town might fall in fright. He, (swift of foot)
Out-ran my purpose: and I return'd then rather
For that I heard the clink, and fall of swords,
And Cassio high in oath: Which till tonight
I ne'er might say before. When I came back
(For this was brief) I found them close together
At blow, and thrust, even as again they were
When you yourself did part them.
More of this matter cannot I report,
But men are men: the best sometimes forget,
Though Cassio did some little wrong to him,
As men in rage strike those that wish them best,
Yet surely Cassio I believe receiv'd
From him that fled, some strange indignity,
Which patience could not pass.

OTHELLO: I know Iago
Thy honesty, and love doth mince this matter,
Making it light to Cassio: Cassio, I love thee,
But never more be Officer of mine.

Enter Desdemona attended.

Look if my gentle Love be not rais'd up:
I'll make thee an example.

DESDEMONA: What is the matter (dear)?

OTHELLO: All 's well, Sweeting:
Come away to bed. Sir for your hurts,
Myself will be your surgeon. Lead him off:
Iago, look with care about the Town,
And silence those whom this vile brawl distracted.
Come Desdemona, 'tis the soldiers' life,
To have their balmy slumbers wak'd with strife.

Exeunt all but Iago and Cassio.

IAGO: What are you hurt Lieutenant?

CASSIO: Ay, past all surgery.

IAGO: Marry God forbid.

CASSIO: Reputation, reputation, reputation: Oh I have lost my reputation. I have lost the immortal part of myself, and what remains is bestial. My reputation, Iago, my reputation.

IAGO: As I am an honest man I had thought you had received some bodily wound; there is more sense in that than in reputation. Reputation is an idle, and most false imposition; oft got without merit, and lost without deserving. You have lost no reputation at all, unless you repute yourself such a loser. What man, there are more ways to recover the General again. You are but now cast in his mood, (a punishment more in policy, than in malice) even so as one would beat his offenceless dog, to affright an imperious lion. Sue to him again, and he 's yours.

CASSIO: I will rather sue to be despis'd, than to deceive so good a Commander, with so slight, so drunken, and so indiscreet an Officer. Drunk? And speak parrot? And squabble? Swagger? Swear? And discourse fustian with one's own shadow? Oh thou invisible spirit of wine, if thou hast no name to be known by, let us call thee devil.

IAGO: What was he that you follow'd with your sword? What had he done to you?

CASSIO: I know not.

IAGO: Is 't possible?

CASSIO: I remember a mass of things, but nothing distinctly: a quarrel, but nothing wherefore. Oh God, that men should put an enemy in their mouths, to steal away their brains? that we should with joy, pleasance, revel and applause, transform ourselves into beasts.

IAGO: Why? But you are now well enough: how came you thus recovered?

CASSIO: It hath pleas'd the devil drunkenness, to give place to the devil wrath, one unperfectness, shows me another to make me frankly despise myself.

IAGO: Come, you are too severe a moraler. As the time, the place, and the condition of this Country stands I could heartily wish this had not befallen: but since it is, as it is, mend it for your own good.

CASSIO: I will ask him for my place again, he shall tell me, I am a drunkard: had I as many mouths as Hydra, such an answer would stop them all. To be now a sensible man, by and by a fool, and presently a beast. Oh strange! Every inordinate cup is unbless'd, and the ingredient is a devil.

IAGO: Come, come: good wine, is a good familiar creature, if it be well us'd: exclaim no more against it. And good Lieutenant, I think, you think I love you.

CASSIO: I have well approved it, Sir. I drunk?

IAGO: You, or any man living, may be drunk at a time man. I tell you what you shall do: Our General's wife, is now the General. I may say so, in this respect, for that he hath devoted, and given up himself to the contemplation, mark: and the devotement of her parts and graces. Confess yourself freely to her: Importune her help to put you in your place again. She is of so free, so kind, so apt, so blessed a disposition, she holds it a vice in her goodness, not to do more than she is requested. This broken joint between you, and her husband, entreat her to splinter. And my fortunes against any lay worth naming, this crack of your love, shall grow stronger, than it was before.

CASSIO: You advise me well.

IAGO: I protest in the sincerity of Love, and honest kindness.

CASSIO: I think it freely: and betimes in the morning, I will beseech the virtuous Desdemona to undertake for me: I am desperate of my fortunes if they check me.

IAGO: You are in the right: good night Lieutenant, I must to the watch.

CASSIO: Good night, honest Iago.

Exit Cassio.

IAGO: And what's he then,
That says I play the villain?
When this advice is free I give, and honest,
Probal to thinking, and indeed the course

To win the Moor again.
For 'tis most easy
Th' inclining Desdemona to subdue
In any honest suit. She's fram'd as fruitful
As the free elements. And then for her
To win the Moor, were to renounce his baptism,
All seals, and symbols of redeemed sin:
His soul is so infetter'd to her love,
That she may make, unmake, do what she list,
Even as her appetite shall play the god,
With his weak function. How am I then a villain,
To counsel Cassio to this parallel course,
Directly to his good? Divinity of hell,
When devils will the blackest sins put on,
They do suggest at first with heavenly shows,
As I do now. For whiles this honest fool
Plies Desdemona, to repair his fortune,
And she for him, pleads strongly to the Moor,
I'll pour this pestilence into his ear:
That she repeals him, for her body's lust,
And by how much she strives to do him good,
She shall undo her credit with the Moor.
So will I turn her virtue into pitch,
And out of her own goodness make the net,
That shall enmesh them all.
How now Roderigo?

Enter Roderigo.

RODERIGO: I do follow here in the chase, not like a hound that hunts, but one that fills up the cry. My money is almost spent; I have been tonight exceedingly well cudgel'd: And I think the issue will be, I shall have so much experience for my pains; And so, with no money at all, and a little more wit, return again to Venice.

IAGO: How poor are they that have not patience?
What wound did ever heal but by degrees?
Thou know'st we work by wit, and not by witchcraft,

And wit depends on dilatory time:
Does 't not go well? Cassio hath beaten thee,
And thou by that small hurt hath cashier'd Cassio:
Though other things grow fair against the Sun,
Yet fruits that blossom first, will first be ripe:
Content thyself, awhile. By the mass, 'tis morning;
Pleasure, and action, make the hours seem short.
Retire thee, go where thou art billeted:
Away, I say, thou shalt know more hereafter:
Nay get thee gone. *Exit Roderigo.*
Two things are to be done:
My wife must move for Cassio to her Mistress:
I'll set her on myself, a while, to draw the Moor apart,
And bring him jump, when he may Cassio find
Soliciting his wife: ay, that 's the way:
Dull not device, by coldness, and delay.

Exit.

III.1

Enter Cassio, Musicians, and Clown.

CASSIO: Masters, play here, I will content your pains, Something that's brief: and bid, good morrow General.

CLOWN: Why Masters, have your instruments been in Naples, that they speak i' th' nose thus?

MUSICIAN: How sir? how?

CLOWN: Are these I pray you, wind instruments?

MUSICIAN: Ay marry are they sir.

CLOWN: Oh, thereby hangs a tale.

MUSICIAN: Whereby hangs a tale, sir?

CLOWN: Marry sir, by many a wind instrument that I know. But Masters, here 's money for you: and the General so likes your music, that he desires you for love's sake to make no more noise with it.

MUSICIAN: Well Sir, we will not.

CLOWN: If you have any music that may not be heard, to 't again. But (as they say) to hear music, the General does not greatly care.

MUSICIAN: We have none such, sir.

CLOWN: Then put up your pipes in your bag, for I'll away. Go, vanish into air, away.

Exeunt Musicians.

CASSIO: Dost thou hear me, mine honest friend?

CLOWN: No, I hear not your honest friend: I hear you.

CASSIO: Prithee keep up thy quillets, there 's a poor piece of gold for thee: if the Gentlewoman that attends the General be stirring, tell her, there 's one Cassio entreats her a little favour of speech. Wilt thou do this?

CLOWN: She is stirring sir: if she will stir hither, I shall seem to notify unto her.

CASSIO: Do, good my friend.

Exit Clown.

Enter Iago.

In happy time, Iago.

IAGO: You have not been a-bed then?

CASSIO: Why no: the day had broke before we parted.
I have made bold (Iago) to send in to your wife;
My suit to her is, that she will to virtuous Desdemona
Procure me some access.

IAGO: I'll send her to you presently:
And I'll devise a mean to draw the Moor
Out of the way, that your converse and business
May be more free. *Exit.*

CASSIO: I humbly thank you for 't. I never knew
A Florentine more kind, and honest.

Enter Emilia.

EMILIA: Good morrow (good Lieutenant) I am sorry
For your displeasure: but all will sure be well.

The General and his wife are talking of it,
And she speaks for you stoutly. The Moor replies,
That he you hurt is of great fame in Cyprus,
And great affinity: and that in wholesome wisdom
He might not but refuse you. But he protests he loves you
And needs no other suitor, but his likings
To take the safest occasion by the front
To bring you in again.

CASSIO: Yet I beseech you,
If you think fit, or that it may be done,
Give me advantage of some brief discourse
With Desdemon alone.

EMILIA: Pray you come in:
I will bestow you where you shall have time
To speak your bosom freely.

CASSIO: I am much bound to you.

Exeunt.

III.2

Enter Othello, Iago, and Gentlemen.

OTHELLO: These letters give (Iago) to the Pilot,
And by him do my duties to the Senate:
That done, I will be walking on the works,
Repair there to me.

IAGO: Well, my good Lord, I'll do 't.

OTHELLO: This fortification (Gentlemen) shall we see 't?

GENTLEMEN: We'll await upon your Lordship.

Exeunt.

III.3

Enter Desdemona, Cassio, and Emilia.

DESDEMONA: Be thou assur'd (good Cassio) I will do
All my abilities in thy behalf.
EMILIA: Good Madam do:
I warrant it grieves my husband,
As if the cause were his.
DESDEMONA: Oh that 's an honest fellow: Do not doubt Cassio
But I will have my Lord, and you again
As friendly as you were.
CASSIO: Bounteous Madam,
Whatever shall become of Michael Cassio,
He 's never anything but your true servant.
DESDEMONA: I know 't: I thank you: you do love my Lord:
You have known him long, and be you well assur'd
He shall in strangeness stand no farther off,
Than in a politic distance.
CASSIO: Ay, but Lady,
That policy may either last so long,
Or feed upon such nice and waterish diet,
Or breed itself so out of circumstances,
That I being absent, and my place suppli'd,
My General will forget my love, and service.
DESDEMONA: Do not doubt that: before Emilia here,
I give thee warrant of thy place. Assure thee,
If I do vow a friendship, I'll perform it
To the last article. My Lord shall never rest,
I'll watch him tame, and talk him out of patience;
His bed shall seem a school, his board a shrift,
I'll intermingle every thing he does
With Cassio's suit: therefore be merry Cassio,

For thy solicitor shall rather die,
Than give thy cause away.

Enter Othello, and Iago.

EMILIA: Madam, here comes my Lord.
CASSIO: Madam, I'll take my leave.
DESDEMONA: Why stay, and hear me speak.
CASSIO: Madam, not now: I am very ill at ease,
Unfit for mine own purposes.
DESDEMONA: Well, do your discretion. *Exit Cassio.*
IAGO: Hah? I like not that.
OTHELLO: What dost thou say?
IAGO: Nothing my Lord; or if – I know not what.
OTHELLO: Was not that Cassio parted from my wife?
IAGO: Cassio my Lord? No sure, I cannot think it
That he would steal away so guilty-like,
Seeing your coming.
OTHELLO: I do believe 'twas he.
DESDEMONA: How now my Lord?
I have been talking with a suitor here,
A man that languishes in your displeasure.
OTHELLO: Who is 't you mean ?
DESDEMONA: Why your Lieutenant Cassio: Good my Lord,
If I have any grace, or power to move you,
His present reconciliation take.
For if he be not one, that truly loves you,
That errs in ignorance, and not in cunning,
I have no judgement in an honest face.
I prithee call him back.
OTHELLO: Went he hence now?
DESDEMONA: Ay sooth; so humbled,
That he hath left part of his grief with me
To suffer with him. Good Love, call him back.
OTHELLO: Not now (sweet Desdemon) some other time.
DESDEMONA: But shall 't be shortly?
OTHELLO: The sooner (Sweet) for you.
DESDEMONA: Shall 't be tonight, at supper?

OTHELLO: No, not tonight.
DESDEMONA: Tomorrow dinner then?
OTHELLO: I shall not dine at home:
I meet the Captains at the Citadel.
DESDEMONA: Why then tomorrow night, on Tuesday morn,
On Tuesday noon, or night; on Wednesday morn.
I prithee name the time, but let it not
Exceed three days. In faith he's penitent:
And yet his trespass, in our common reason
(Save that they say the wars must make example)
Out of her best, is not almost a fault
T' incur a private check. When shall he come?
Tell me Othello. I wonder in my soul
What you would ask me, that I should deny,
Or stand so mamm'ring on? What? Michael Cassio,
That came a-wooing with you? and so many a time
(When I have spoke of you dispraisingly)
Hath ta'en your part, to have so much to do
To bring him in? Birlady, I could do much.
OTHELLO: Prithee no more: Let him come when he will:
I will deny thee nothing.
DESDEMONA: Why, this is not a boon:
'Tis as I should entreat you wear your gloves,
Or feed on nourishing dishes, or keep you warm,
Or sue to you, to do a peculiar profit
To your own person. Nay, when I have a suit
Wherein I mean to touch your love indeed.
It shall be full of poise, and difficult weight,
And fearful to be granted.
OTHELLO: I will deny thee nothing.
Whereon, I do beseech thee, grant me this,
To leave me but a little to myself.
DESDEMONA: Shall I deny you? No: farewell my Lord.
OTHELLO: Farewell my Desdemona, I'll come to thee straight.
DESDEMONA: Emilia come; be as your fancies teach you:
Whate'er you be, I am obedient.

Exeunt Desdemona and Emilia.

OTHELLO: Excellent wretch: Perdition catch my soul
But I do love thee: and when I love thee not,
Chaos is come again.

IAGO: My noble Lord.

OTHELLO: What dost thou say, Iago?

IAGO: Did Michael Cassio
When he woo'd my Lady, know of your love?

OTHELLO: He did, from first to last:
Why dost thou ask?

IAGO: But for a satisfaction of my thought,
No further harm.

OTHELLO: Why of thy thought, Iago?

IAGO: I did not think he had been acquainted with her.

OTHELLO: O yes, and went between us very oft.

IAGO: Indeed?

OTHELLO: Indeed? Ay indeed. Discern'st thou aught in that?
Is he not honest?

IAGO: Honest, my Lord?

OTHELLO: Honest? Ay honest,

IAGO: My Lord, for aught I know.

OTHELLO: What dost thou think?

IAGO: Think, my Lord?

OTHELLO: Think, my Lord? By Heaven, thou echo'st me;
As if there were some Monster in thy thought
Too hideous to be shown. Thou didst mean something:
I heard thee say even now, thou lik'st not that,
When Cassio left my wife. What didst not like?
And when I told thee, he was of my counsel,
Of my whole course of wooing; thou criedst, Indeed?
And didst contract, and purse thy brow together,
As if thou then hadst shut up in thy brain
Some horrible conceit. If thou dost love me,
Show me thy thought.

IAGO: My Lord, you know I love you.

OTHELLO: I think thou dost:

And for I know thou 'rt full of love, and honesty,
And weigh'st thy words before thou giv'st them breath,
Therefore these stops of thine, fright me the more:
For such things in a false disloyal knave
Are tricks of custom: but in a man that 's just,
They're close dilations, working from the heart,
That passion cannot rule.

IAGO: For Michael Cassio,
I dare be sworn, I think that he is honest.

OTHELLO: I think so too.

IAGO: Men should be what they seem,
Or those that be not, would they might seem none.

OTHELLO: Certain, men should be what they seem.

IAGO: Why then I think Cassio 's an honest man.

OTHELLO: Nay, yet there 's more in this?
I prithee speak to me, as to thy thinkings,
As thou dost ruminate, and give thy worst of thoughts
The worst of words.

IAGO: Good my Lord pardon me,
Though I am bound to every act of duty,
I am not bound to that: All slaves are free:
Utter my thoughts? Why say, they are vile, and false?
As where 's that Palace, whereinto foul things
Sometimes intrude not? Who has that breast so pure,
Wherein uncleanly apprehensions
Keep leets, and law-days, and in sessions sit
With meditations lawful?

OTHELLO: Thou dost conspire against thy friend (Iago)
If thou but think'st him wrong'd, and mak'st his car
A stranger to thy thoughts.

IAGO: I do beseech you,
Though I perchance am vicious in my guess
(As I confess it is my nature's plague
To spy into abuses, and of my jealousy
Shapes faults that are not) that your wisdom

From one, that so imperfectly conceits,
Would take no notice, nor build yourself a trouble
Out of his scattering, and unsure observance:
It were not for your quiet, nor your good,
Nor for my manhood, honesty, and wisdom,
To let you know my thoughts.

OTHELLO: What dost thou mean?

IAGO: Good name in man, and woman (dear my Lord)
Is the immediate jewel of their souls;
Who steals my purse, steals trash:
'Tis something, nothing;
'Twas mine, 'tis his, and has been slave to thousands:
But he that filches from me my good name,
Robs me of that, which not enriches him,
And makes me poor indeed.

OTHELLO: By Heaven I'll know thy thoughts.

IAGO: You cannot, if my heart were in your hand,
Nor shall not, whilst 'tis in my custody.

OTHELLO: Ha?

IAGO: Oh, beware my Lord, of jealousy,
It is the green-ey'd Monster, which doth mock
The meat it feeds on. That cuckold lives in bliss,
Who certain of his fate, loves not his wronger:
But oh, what damned minutes tells he o'er,
Who dotes, yet doubts: Suspects, yet soundly loves?

OTHELLO: O misery.

IAGO: Poor, and content, is rich, and rich enough,
But riches fineless, is as poor as Winter,
To him that ever fears he shall be poor:
Good God, the souls of all my tribe defend
From jealousy.

OTHELLO: Why? why is this?
Think'st thou, I'ld make a life of jealousy;
To follow still the changes of the Moon
With fresh suspicions? No: to be once in doubt,
Is once to be resolv'd: Exchange me for a goat,

When I shall turn the business of my soul
To such exsufflicate, and blown surmises,
Matching thy inference. 'Tis not to make me jealous,
To say my wife is fair, feeds well, loves company,
Is free of speech, sings, plays, and dances:
Where virtue is, these are more virtuous.
Nor from mine own weak merits, will I draw
The smallest fear, or doubt of her revolt,
For she had eyes, and chose me. No Iago,
I'll see before I doubt; when I doubt, prove;
And on the proof, there is no more but this,
Away at once with love, or jealousy.

IAGO: I am glad of this: For now I shall have reason
To show the love and duty that I bear you
With franker spirit. Therefore (as I am bound)
Receive it from me. I speak not yet of proof:
Look to your wife, observe her well with Cassio,
Wear your eyes, thus: not jealous, nor secure:
I would not have your free, and noble nature,
Out of self-bounty, be abus'd: Look to 't:
I know our country disposition well:
In Venice, they do let God see the pranks
They dare not show their husbands.
Their best conscience,
Is not to leave 't undone, but keep 't unknown.

OTHELLO: Dost thou say so?

IAGO: She did deceive her Father, marrying you,
And when she seem'd to shake, and fear your looks,
She lov'd them most.

OTHELLO: And so she did.

IAGO: Why go to then:
She that so young could give out such a seeming
To seel her Father's eyes up, close as oak,
He thought 'twas witchcraft.
But I am much to blame:
I humbly do beseech you of your pardon

For too much loving you.
OTHELLO: I am bound to thee for ever.
IAGO: I see this hath a little dash'd your spirits.
OTHELLO: Not a jot, not a jot.
IAGO: I' faith I fear it has:
I hope you will consider what is spoke
Comes from your love.
But I do see y' are mov'd:
I am to pray you, not to strain my speech
To grosser issues, nor to larger reach,
Than to suspicion.
OTHELLO: I will not.
IAGO: Should you do so (my Lord)
My speech should fall into such vile success,
Which my thoughts aim'd not.
Cassio 's my worthy friend:
My Lord, I see y' are mov'd.
OTHELLO: No, not much mov'd:
I do not think but Desdemona's honest.
IAGO: Long live she so;
And long live you to think so.
OTHELLO: And yet how Nature erring from itself.
IAGO: Ay, there 's the point:
As (to be bold with you)
Not to affect many proposed matches
Of her own clime, complexion, and degree,
Whereto we see in all things, Nature tends:
Foh, one may smell in such, a will most rank,
Foul disproportions, thoughts unnatural.
But (pardon me) I do not in position
Distinctly speak of her, though I may fear
Her will, recoiling to her better judgement,
May fall to match you with her country forms,
And happily repent.
OTHELLO: Farewell, farewell:
If more thou dost perceive, let me know more:

Set on thy wife to observe.
Leave me Iago.
IAGO: My Lord, I take my leave.
OTHELLO: Why did I marry?
This honest creature (doubtless)
Sees, and knows more, much more than he unfolds.
IAGO: My Lord, I would I might entreat your Honour
To scan this thing no farther: Leave it to time,
Although 'tis fit that Cassio have his place;
For sure he fills it up with great ability;
Yet if you please, to hold him off awhile:
You shall by that perceive him, and his means:
Note if your Lady strain his entertainment
With any strong, or vehement importunity,
Much will be seen in that: In the mean time,
Let me be thought too busy in my fears,
(As worthy cause I have to fear I am)
And hold her free, I do beseech your Honour.
OTHELLO: Fear not my government.
IAGO: I once more take my leave. *Exit.*
OTHELLO: This fellow 's of exceeding honesty,
And knows all quantities with a learn'd spirit
Of human dealings. If I do prove her haggard,
Though that her jesses were my dear heart-strings,
I'ld whistle her off, and let her down the wind
To prey at Fortune. Haply, for I am black,
And have not those soft parts of conversation
That chamberers have: Or for I am declin'd
Into the vale of years (yet that 's not much)
She 's gone. I am abus'd, and my relief
Must be to loathe her. Oh curse of marriage!
That we can call these delicate creatures ours,
And not their appetites! I had rather be a toad,
And live upon the vapour of a dungeon,
Than keep a corner in the thing I love
For others' uses. Yet 'tis the plague to Great-ones,

Prerogativ'd are they less than the base,
'Tis destiny unshunnable, like death:
Even then, this forked plague is fated to us,
When we do quicken. Look where she comes:

Enter Desdemona and Emilia.

If she be false, Heaven mock'd itself:
I'll not believe 't.

DESDEMONA: How now, my dear Othello?
Your dinner, and the generous Islanders
By you invited, do attend your presence.

OTHELLO: I am to blame.

DESDEMONA: Why do you speak so faintly?
Are you not well?

OTHELLO: I have a pain upon my forehead, here.

DESDEMONA: Faith that 's with watching, 'twill away again.
Let me but bind it hard, within this hour
It will be well.

OTHELLO: Your napkin is too little:
Let it alone: Come, I'll go in with you.

DESDEMONA: I am very sorry that you are not well.

Exeunt Othello and Desdemona.

EMILIA: I am glad I have found this napkin:
This was her first remembrance from the Moor,
My wayward husband hath a hundred times
Woo'd me to steal it. But she so loves the token,
(For he conjur'd her, she should ever keep it)
That she reserves it evermore about her,
To kiss, and talk to. I'll have the work ta'en out,
And give 't Iago: what he will do with it
Heaven knows, not I:
I nothing, but to please his fantasy.

Enter Iago.

IAGO: How now? What do you here alone?

EMILIA: Do not you chide: I have a thing for you.

IAGO: You have a thing for me?
It is a common thing –

EMILIA: Hah?
IAGO: To have a foolish wife.
EMILIA: Oh, is that all? What will you give me now
For that same handkerchief?
IAGO: What handkerchief?
EMILIA: What handkerchief?
Why that the Moor first gave to Desdemona,
That which so often you did bid me steal.
IAGO: Hast stolen it from her?
EMILIA: No faith, she let it drop by negligence,
And to th' advantage, I being here, took 't up:
Look, here 'tis.
IAGO: A good wench, give it me.
EMILIA: What will you do with 't, that you have been so earnest to have me filch it ?
IAGO: Why, what is that to you?
EMILIA: If it be not for some purpose of import,
Give 't me again. Poor Lady, she'll run mad
When she shall lack it.
IAGO: Be not acknown on 't:
I have use for it. Go, leave me. *Exit Emilia.*
I will in Cassio's lodging lose this napkin,
And let him find it. Trifles light as air,
Are to the jealous, confirmations strong,
As proofs of holy Writ. This may do something.
The Moor already changes with my poison:
Dangerous conceits, are in their natures poisons,
Which at the first are scarce found to distaste:
But with a little act upon the blood,
Burn like the mines of sulphur. I did say so.

Enter Othello.

Look where he comes: Not poppy, nor mandragora,
Nor all the drowsy syrups of the world
Shall ever medicine thee to that sweet sleep
Which thou ow'dst yesterday.
OTHELLO: Ha, ha, false to me?

IAGO: Why how now General? No more of that.
OTHELLO: Avaunt, be gone: Thou has set me on the rack:
    I swear 'tis better to be much abus'd,
    Than but to know 't a little.
IAGO: How now, my Lord?
OTHELLO: What sense had I, in her stol'n hours of lust?
    I saw 't not, thought it not: it harm'd not me:
    I slept the next night well, fed well, was free, and merry.
    I found not Cassio's kisses on her lips:
    He that is robb'd, not wanting what is stol'n,
    Let him not know 't, and he 's not robb'd at all.
IAGO: I am sorry to hear this!
OTHELLO: I had been happy, if the general camp,
    Pioners and all, had tasted her sweet body,
    So I had nothing known. Oh now, for ever
    Farewell the tranquil mind; farewell content;
    Farewell the plumed troops, and the big wars,
    That makes ambition, virtue! Oh farewell,
    Farewell the neighing steed, and the shrill trump,
    The spirit-stirring drum, th' ear-piercing fife,
    The royal banner, and all quality,
    Pride, pomp, and circumstance of glorious War:
    And O you mortal engines, whose rude throats
    Th' immortal Jove's dread clamours, counterfeit,
    Farewell: Othello's occupation 's gone.
IAGO: Is 't possible my Lord?
OTHELLO: Villain, be sure thou prove my Love a whore;
    Be sure of it: Give me the ocular proof,
    Or by the worth of mine eternal soul,
    Thou hadst been better have been born a dog
    Than answer my wak'd wrath.
IAGO: Is 't come to this?
OTHELLO: Make me to see't: or (at the least) so prove it,
    That the probation bear no hinge, nor loop,
    To hang a doubt on: Or woe upon thy life.
IAGO: My noble Lord.

OTHELLO: If thou dost slander her, and torture me,
Never pray more: Abandon all remorse;
On horror's head, horrors accumulate:
Do deeds to make Heaven weep, all Earth amaz'd;
For nothing canst thou to damnation add,
Greater than that.
IAGO: O Grace! O Heaven forgive me!
Are you a man? Have you a soul? or sense?
God buy you: take mine office. Oh wretched fool,
That lov'st to make thine honesty, a vice!
Oh monstrous world! Take note, take note (O World)
To be direct and honest, is not safe.
I thank you for this profit, and from hence
I'll love no friend, sith love breeds such offence.
OTHELLO: Nay stay: thou shouldst be honest.
IAGO: I should be wise; for honesty 's a fool,
And loses that it works for.
OTHELLO: By the World,
I think my wife be honest, and think she is not:
I think that thou art just, and think thou art not:
I'll have some proof. My name that was as fresh
As Dian's visage, is now begrim'd and black
As mine own face. If there be cords, or knives,
Poison, or fire, or suffocating streams,
I'll not endure it. Would I were satisfied.
IAGO: I see you are eaten up with passion:
I do repent me, that I put it to you.
You would be satisfied?
OTHELLO: Would? Nay, and I will.
IAGO: And may: but how? How satisfied, my Lord?
Would you the supervision grossly gape on?
Behold her topp'd?
OTHELLO: Death, and damnation. Oh!
IAGO: It were a tedious difficulty, I think,
To bring them to that prospect: Damn them then,
If ever mortal eyes do see them bolster

More than their own. What then? How then?
What shall I say? Where 's satisfaction?
It is impossible you should see this,
Were they as prime as goats, as hot as monkeys,
As salt as wolves in pride, and fools as gross
As ignorance, made drunk. But yet, I say,
If imputation, and strong circumstances,
Which lead directly to the door of Truth,
Will give you satisfaction, you might have 't.
OTHELLO: Give me a living reason she's disloyal.
IAGO: I do not like the office.
But sith I am enter'd in this cause so far
(Prick'd to 't by foolish honesty, and love)
I will go on. I lay with Cassio lately,
And being troubled with a raging tooth,
I could not sleep. There are a kind of men,
So loose of soul, that in their sleeps will mutter
Their affairs: one of this kind is Cassio:
In sleep I heard him say, sweet Desdemona,
Let us be wary, let us hide our loves,
And then (Sir) would he gripe, and wring my hand:
Cry, oh sweet creature: then kiss me hard,
As if he pluck'd up kisses by the roots,
That grew upon my lips, laid his leg over my thigh,
And sigh, and kiss, and then cry cursed Fate,
That gave thee to the Moor.
OTHELLO: O monstrous! monstrous!
IAGO: Nay, this was but his dream.
OTHELLO: But this denoted a foregone conclusion,
'Tis a shrewd doubt, though it be but a dream.
IAGO: And this may help to thicken other proofs,
That do demonstrate thinly.
OTHELLO: I'll tear her all to pieces.
IAGO: Nay yet be wise; yet we see nothing done,
She may be honest yet: Tell me but this,
Have you not sometimes seen a handkerchief

Spotted with strawberries, in your wife's hand?
OTHELLO: I gave her such a one: 'twas my first gift.
IAGO: I know not that: but such a handkerchief
(I am sure it was your wife's) did I today
See Cassio wipe his beard with.
OTHELLO: If it be that.
IAGO: If it be that, or any, it was hers,
It speaks against her with the other proofs.
OTHELLO: O that the slave had forty thousand lives:
One is too poor, too weak for my revenge.
Now do I see 'tis true. Look here Iago,
All my fond love thus do I blow to Heaven. 'Tis gone.
Arise black vengeance, from the hollow hell,
Yield up (O Love) thy crown, and hearted throne
To tyrannous hate. Swell bosom with thy fraught,
For 'tis of aspics' tongues.
IAGO: Yet be content.
OTHELLO: Oh blood, blood, blood.
IAGO: Patience I say: your mind may change.
OTHELLO: Never Iago. Like to the Pontic Sea,
Whose icy current, and compulsive course,
Ne'er keeps retiring ebb, but keeps due on
To the Propontic, and the Hellespont:
Even so my bloody thoughts, with violent pace
Shall ne'er look back, ne'er ebb to humble love
Till that a capable, and wide revenge
Swallow them up. Now by yond marble Heaven,
In the due reverence of a sacred vow,
I here engage my words.
IAGO: Do not rise yet:
Witness you ever-burning lights above,
You elements, that clip us round about, *Iago kneels.*
Witness that here Iago doth give up
The execution of his wit, hands, heart,
To wrong'd Othello's service. Let him command,
And to obey shall be in me remorse,

What bloody business ever.

OTHELLO: I greet thy love,
Not with vain thanks, but with acceptance bounteous,
And will upon the instant put thee to 't.
Within these three days let me hear thee say,
That Cassio 's not alive.

IAGO: My friend is dead:
'Tis done at your request.
But let her live.

OTHELLO: Damn her lewd minx:
O damn her, damn her.
Come go with me apart, I will withdraw
To furnish me with some swift means of death
For the fair Devil.
Now art thou my Lieutenant.

IAGO: I am your own for ever.

Exeunt.

III.4

Enter Desdemona, Emilia, and Clown.

DESDEMONA: Do you know Sirrah, where Lieutenant Cassio lies?

CLOWN: I dare not say he lies any where.

DESDEMONA: Why man?

CLOWN: He 's a soldier, and for me to say a soldier lies, 'tis stabbing.

DESDEMONA: Go to: where lodges he?

CLOWN: To tell you where he lodges, is to tell you where I lie.

DESDEMONA: Can any thing be made of this?

CLOWN: I know not where he lodges, and for me to devise a lodging, and say he lies here, or he lies there, were to lie in mine own throat.

DESDEMONA: Can you inquire him out? and be edified by report?

CLOWN: I will catechize the world for him, that is, make questions, and by them answer.

DESDEMONA: Seek him, bid him come hither: tell him, I have mov'd my Lord on his behalf, and hope all will be well.

CLOWN: To do this, is within the compass of man's wit, and therefore I will attempt the doing it.

Exit Clown.

DESDEMONA: Where should I lose the handkerchief, Emilia?

EMILIA: I know not Madam.

DESDEMONA: Believe me, I had rather have lost my purse
Full of crusadoes. And but my noble Moor
Is true of mind, and made of no such baseness,
As jealous creatures are, it were enough
To put him to ill thinking.

EMILIA: Is he not jealous?

DESDEMONA: Who, he? I think the Sun where he was born,
Drew all such humours from him.

EMILIA: Look where he comes.

Enter Othello.

DESDEMONA: I will not leave him now, till Cassio
Be call'd to him. How is 't with you, my Lord?

OTHELLO: Well my good Lady. Oh hardness to dissemble!
How do you, Desdemona?

DESDEMONA: Well, my good Lord.

OTHELLO: Give me your hand.
This hand is moist my Lady.

DESDEMONA: It hath felt no age, nor known no sorrow.

OTHELLO: This argues fruitfulness, and liberal heart:
Hot, hot, and moist. This hand of yours requires
A sequester from liberty: fasting, and prayer,
Much castigation, exercise devout,
For here 's a young, and sweating devil here
That commonly rebels: 'Tis a good hand,
A frank one.

DESDEMONA: You may (indeed) say so:
For 'twas that hand that gave away my heart.
OTHELLO: A liberal hand. The hearts of old, gave hands:
But our new heraldry is hands, not hearts.
DESDEMONA: I cannot speak of this:
Come, now your promise.
OTHELLO: What promise, Chuck?
DESDEMONA: I have sent to bid Cassio come speak with you.
OTHELLO: I have a salt and sorry rheum offends me:
Lend me thy handkerchief.
DESDEMONA: Here my Lord.
OTHELLO: That which I gave you.
DESDEMONA: I have it not about me.
OTHELLO: Not?
DESDEMONA: No indeed, my Lord.
OTHELLO: That 's a fault: That handkerchief
Did an Egyptian to my Mother give:
She was a charmer, and could almost read
The thoughts of people. She told her, while she kept it,
'Twould make her amiable, and subdue my father
Entirely to her love: But if she lost it,
Or made a gift of it, my Father's eye
Should hold her loathed, and his spirits should hunt
After new fancies. She dying, gave it me,
And bid me (when my Fate would have me wiv'd),
To give it her. I did so; and take heed on 't,
Make it a darling, like your precious eye:
To lose 't, or give 't away, were such perdition,
As nothing else could match.
DESDEMONA: Is 't possible?
OTHELLO: 'Tis true: There 's magic in the web of it:
A Sibyl that had number'd in the world
The Sun to course, two hundred compasses,
In her prophetic fury sew'd the work:
The worms were hallow'd, that did breed the silk,
And it was dyed in mummy, which the skilful

Conserv'd of maidens' hearts.
DESDEMONA: Indeed? Is 't true?
OTHELLO: Most veritable, therefore look to 't well.
DESDEMONA: Then would to God, that I had never seen 't!
OTHELLO: Ha? wherefore?
DESDEMONA: Why do you speak so startingly, and rash?
OTHELLO: Is 't lost? Is 't gone? Speak, is it out o' th' way?
DESDEMONA: Bless us.
OTHELLO: Say you?
DESDEMONA: It is not lost: but what and if it were?
OTHELLO: How?
DESDEMONA: I say it is not lost.
OTHELLO: Fetch 't, let me see 't.
DESDEMONA: Why so I can: but I will not now:
This is a trick to put me from my suit,
Pray you let Cassio be receiv'd again.
OTHELLO: Fetch me the handkerchief,
My mind misgives.
DESDEMONA: Come, come: You'll never meet a more sufficient man.
OTHELLO: The handkerchief.
DESDEMONA: A man that all his time
Hath founded his good fortunes on your love;
Shar'd dangers with you.
OTHELLO: The handkerchief.
DESDEMONA: In sooth you are to blame.
OTHELLO: Zounds.

Exit Othello.

EMILIA: Is not this man jealous?
DESDEMONA: I ne'er saw this before.
Sure, there 's some wonder in this handkerchief,
I am most unhappy in the loss of it.
EMILIA: 'Tis not a year or two shows us a man:
They are all but stomachs, and we all but food.
They eat us hungerly, and when they are full
They belch us.

Enter Iago and Cassio.

Look you, Cassio and my husband.

IAGO: There is no other way: 'tis she must do 't;
And lo the happiness: go, and importune her.

DESDEMONA: How now (good Cassio) what 's the news with you?

CASSIO: Madam, my former suit. I do beseech you,
That by your virtuous means, I may again
Exist, and be a member of his love,
Whom I, with all the office of my heart
Entirely honour, I would not be delay'd.
If my offence, be of such mortal kind,
That nor my service past, nor present sorrows,
Nor purpos'd merit in futurity,
Can ransom me into his love again,
But to know so, must be my benefit:
So shall I clothe me in a forc'd content,
And shut myself up in some other course
To Fortune's alms.

DESDEMONA: Alas (thrice-gentle Cassio)
My advocation is not now in tune;
My Lord, is not my Lord; nor should I know him,
Were he in favour, as in humour alter'd.
So help me every spirit sanctified,
As I have spoken for you all my best,
And stood within the blank of his displeasure
For my free speech. You must awhile be patient:
What I can do, I will: and more I will
Than for myself, I dare. Let that suffice you.

IAGO: Is my Lord angry?

EMILIA: He went hence but now:
And certainly in strange unquietness.

IAGO: Can he be angry? I have seen the cannon
When it hath blown his ranks into the air,
And like the Devil from his very arm
Puff'd his own brother: And he is angry?

Something of moment then: I will go meet him,
There 's matter in 't indeed, if he be angry. *Exit.*

DESDEMONA: I prithee do so. Something sure of state,
Either from Venice, or some unhatch'd practice
Made demonstrable here in Cyprus, to him,
Hath puddled his clear spirit: and in such cases,
Men's natures wrangle with inferior things,
Though great ones are their object. 'Tis even so.
For let our finger ache, and it indues
Our other healthful members, even to a sense
Of pain. Nay, we must think men are not Gods,
Nor of them look for such observancy
As fits the bridal. Beshrew me much, Emilia,
I was (unhandsome warrior, as I am)
Arraigning his unkindness with my soul:
But now I find, I had suborn'd the witness,
And he 's indicted falsely.

EMILIA: Pray heaven it be
State matters, as you think, and no conception,
Nor no jealous toy, concerning you.

DESDEMONA: Alas the day, I never gave him cause.

EMILIA: But jealous souls will not be answer'd so;
They are not ever jealous for the cause,
But jealous, for they 're jealous. It is a Monster
Begot upon itself, born on itself.

DESDEMONA: Heaven keep the Monster from Othello's mind.

EMILIA: Lady, Amen.

DESDEMONA: I will go seek him. Cassio, walk here about:
If I do find him fit, I'll move your suit,
And seek to effect it to my uttermost.

Exeunt Desdemona and Emilia.

CASSIO: I humbly thank your Ladyship.

Enter Bianca.

BIANCA: 'Save you (friend Cassio).

CASSIO: What make you from home?
How is 't with you, my most fair Bianca?

Indeed (sweet Love) I was coming to your house.
BIANCA: And I was going to your lodging, Cassio.
What? keep a week away? Seven days, and nights?
Eight score eight hours? And lovers' absent hours
More tedious than the dial, eight score times?
Oh weary reckoning.
CASSIO: Pardon me, Bianca:
I have this while with leaden thoughts been press'd,
But I shall in a more continuate time
Strike off this score of absence. Sweet Bianca
Take me this work out.
BIANCA: Oh Cassio, whence came this?
This is some token from a newer friend,
To the felt absence: now I feel a cause:
Is 't come to this? Well, well.
CASSIO: Go to, woman:
Throw your vile guesses in the Devil's teeth,
From whence you have them. You are jealous now,
That this is from some Mistress, some remembrance;
No, in good troth Bianca.
BIANCA: Why, whose is it?
CASSIO: I know not neither:
I found it in my chamber,
I like the work well; Ere it be demanded
(As like enough it will) I would have it copied:
Take it, and do 't, and leave me for this time.
BIANCA: Leave you? Wherefore?
CASSIO: I do attend here on the General,
And think it no addition, nor my wish
To have him see me woman'd.
BIANCA: Why, I pray you?
CASSIO: Not that I love you not.
BIANCA: But that you do not love me.
I pray you bring me on the way a little,
And say, if I shall see you soon at night?
CASSIO: 'Tis but a little way that I can bring you,

For I attend here: But I'll see you soon.
BIANCA: 'Tis very good: I must be circumstanc'd.
Exeunt.

IV.1

Enter Othello, and Iago.

IAGO: Will you think so?
OTHELLO: Think so, Iago?
IAGO: What, to kiss in private?
OTHELLO: An unauthoriz'd kiss?
IAGO: Or to be naked with her friend in bed,
An hour, or more, not meaning any harm?
OTHELLO: Naked in bed (Iago) and not mean harm?
It is hypocrisy against the Devil:
They that mean virtuously, and yet do so,
The Devil their virtue tempts, and they tempt Heaven.
IAGO: If they do nothing, 'tis a venial slip:
But if I give my wife a handkerchief.
OTHELLO: What then?
IAGO: Why then 'tis hers (my Lord) and being hers,
She may (I think) bestow 't on any man.
OTHELLO: She is protectress of her honour too:
May she give that?
IAGO: Her honour is an essence that 's not seen,
They have it very oft, that have it not.
But for the handkerchief.
OTHELLO: By heaven, I would most gladly have forgot it:
Thou said'st (oh, it comes o'er my memory,
As doth the raven o'er the infectious house:
Boding to all) he had my handkerchief.
IAGO: Ay: what of that?

OTHELLO: That 's not so good now.
IAGO: What if I had said, I had seen him do you wrong?
  Or heard him say (as knaves be such abroad,
  Who having by their own importunate suit,
  Or voluntary dotage of some Mistress,
  Convinced or suppli'd them, cannot choose
  But they must blab.)
OTHELLO: Hath he said anything?
IAGO: He hath (my Lord) but be you well assur'd,
  No more than he'll unswear.
OTHELLO: What hath he said?
IAGO: Faith, that he did: I know not what he did.
OTHELLO: What? What?
IAGO: Lie.
OTHELLO: With her?
IAGO: With her? On her: what you will.
OTHELLO: Lie with her? lie on her? We say lie on her, when they be-lie-her. Lie with her: 'zounds, that 's fulsome: Handkerchief: Confessions: Handkerchief. To confess, and be hang'd for his labour. First, to be hang'd, and then to confess: I tremble at it. Nature would not invest herself in such shadowing passion, without some instruction. It is not words that shakes me thus, (pish) noses, ears, and lips: is 't possible. Confess? Handkerchief? O devil. *Falls in a trance.*
IAGO: Work on,
  My medicine works. Thus credulous fools are caught,
  And many worthy, and chaste dames even thus,
  (All guiltless) meet reproach: what hoa? My Lord?
  My Lord, I say: Othello.

Enter Cassio.

  How now Cassio?
CASSIO: What 's the matter?
IAGO: My Lord is fall'n into an epilepsy,
  This is his second fit: he had one yesterday.
CASSIO: Rub him about the temples.
IAGO: No forbear,
  The lethargy must have his quiet course:

If not, he foams at mouth: and by and by
Breaks out to savage madness. Look, he stirs:
Do you withdraw yourself a little while,
He will recover straight: when he is gone,
I would on great occasion, speak with you.
Exit Cassio.

How is it General? Have you not hurt your head?
OTHELLO: Dost thou mock me?
IAGO: I mock you not, by Heaven:
Would you would bear your fortune like a man.
OTHELLO: A horned man 's a monster, and a beast.
IAGO: There 's many a beast then in a populous city,
And many a civil monster.
OTHELLO: Did he confess it?
IAGO: Good sir, be a man:
Think every bearded fellow that 's but yok'd
May draw with you. There 's millions now alive,
That nightly lie in those unproper beds,
Which they dare swear peculiar. Your case is better.
Oh, 'tis the spite of hell, the Fiend's arch-mock,
To lip a wanton in a secure couch;
And to suppose her chaste. No, let me know,
And knowing what I am, I know what she shall be.
OTHELLO: Oh, thou art wise: 'tis certain.
IAGO: Stand you awhile apart,
Confine yourself but in a patient list,
Whilst you were here, o'erwhelmed with your grief
(A passion most unsuiting such a man)
Cassio came hither. I shifted him away,
And laid good 'scuses upon your ecstasy,
Bad him anon return: and here speak with me,
The which he promis'd. Do but encave yourself,
And mark the fleers, the gibes, and notable scorns
That dwell in every region of his face;
For I will make him tell the tale anew;
Where, how, how oft, how long ago, and when

He hath, and is again to cope your wife.
I say, but mark his gesture: marry patience,
Or I shall say y' are all in all in spleen,
And nothing of a man.

OTHELLO: Dost thou hear, Iago,
I will be found most cunning in my patience:
But (dost thou hear) most bloody.

IAGO: That 's not amiss,
But yet keep time in all: will you withdraw?
[*Othello hides himself.*]
Now will I question Cassio of Bianca,
A housewife that by selling her desires
Buys herself bread, and cloth. It is a creature
That dotes on Cassio, (as 'tis the strumpet's plague
To beguile many, and be beguil'd by one)
He, when he hears of her, cannot restrain
From the excess of laughter. Here he comes.
Enter Cassio.
As he shall smile, Othello shall go mad:
And his unbookish jealousy must conserve
Poor Cassio's smiles, gestures, and light behaviours
Quite in the wrong. How do you Lieutenant?

CASSIO: The worser, than you give me the addition,
Whose want even kills me.

IAGO: Ply Desdemona well, and you are sure on 't:
Now, if this suit lay in Bianca's dower,
How quickly should you speed?

CASSIO: Alas poor caitiff.

OTHELLO: Look how he laughs already.

IAGO: I never knew woman love man so.

CASSIO: Alas poor rogue, I think i' faith she loves me.

OTHELLO: Now he denies it faintly: and laughs it out.

IAGO: Do you hear Cassio?

OTHELLO: Now he importunes him
To tell it o'er: go to, well said, well said.

IAGO: She gives it out, that you shall marry her.

Do you intend it?

CASSIO: Ha, ha, ha.

OTHELLO: Do ye triumph, Roman? do you triumph?

CASSIO: I marry. What? A customer; prithee bear
Some charity to my wit, do not think it
So unwholesome. Ha, ha, ha.

OTHELLO: So, so, so, so: they laugh, that wins.

IAGO: Faith the cry goes, that you marry her.

CASSIO: Prithee say true.

IAGO: I am a very villain else.

OTHELLO: Have you scor'd me? Well.

CASSIO: This is the monkey's own giving out:
She is persuaded I will marry her
Out of her own love and flattery, not out of my promise.

OTHELLO: Iago beckons me: now he begins the story.

CASSIO: She was here even now: she haunts me in every place. I was the other day talking on the sea-bank with certain Venetians, and thither comes the bauble, by this hand she falls me thus about my neck.

OTHELLO: Crying oh dear Cassio, as it were: his gesture imports it.

CASSIO: So hangs, and lolls, and weeps upon me:
So shakes, and pulls me. Ha, ha, ha.

OTHELLO: Now he tells how she pluck'd him to my chamber: oh, I see that nose of yours, but not that dog, I shall throw it to.

CASSIO: Well, I must leave her company.

IAGO: Before me: look where she comes.

Enter Bianca.

CASSIO: 'Tis such another fitchew: marry a perfum'd one?
What do you mean by this haunting of me?

BIANCA: Let the devil, and his dam haunt you: what did you mean by that same handkerchief, you gave me even now? I was a fine fool to take it: I must take out the work? A likely piece of work, that you should find it in your chamber, and know not who left it there. This is some minx's token, and I must take out the work? There, give it your hobbyhorse, wheresoever you had it, I'll take out no work on 't.

CASSIO: How now, my sweet Bianca?
How now? How now?

OTHELLO: By Heaven, that should be my handkerchief.

BIANCA: If you'll come to supper tonight you may, if you will not, come when you are next prepar'd for. *Exit.*

IAGO: After her: after her.

CASSIO: Faith I must, she'll rail in the streets else.

IAGO: Will you sup there?

CASSIO: Faith I intend so.

IAGO: Well, I may chance to see you: for I would very fain speak with you.

CASSIO: Prithee come: will you?

IAGO: Go to, say no more. *Exit Cassio.*

OTHELLO: How shall I murther him, Iago.

IAGO: Did you perceive how he laugh'd at his vice?

OTHELLO: Oh, Iago.

IAGO: And did you see the handkerchief?

OTHELLO: Was that mine?

IAGO: Yours by this hand: and to see how he prizes the foolish woman your wife: she gave it him, and he hath given it his whore.

OTHELLO: I would have him nine years a killing:
A fine woman, a fair woman, a sweet woman!

IAGO: Nay, you must forget that.

OTHELLO: Ay, let her rot and perish, and be damn'd to-night, for she shall not live. No, my heart is turn'd to stone: I strike it, and it hurts my hand. Oh, the world hath not a sweeter creature: she might lie by an Emperor's side, and command him tasks.

IAGO: Nay, that 's not your way.

OTHELLO: Hang her, I do but say what she is: so delicate with her needle: an admirable musician. Oh she will sing the savageness out of a bear: of so high and plenteous wit, and invention!

IAGO: She 's the worse for all this.

OTHELLO: Oh, a thousand, a thousand times: And then be of so gentle a condition!

IAGO: Ay too gentle.

OTHELLO: Nay that 's certain:
But yet the pity of it, Iago: oh Iago, the pity of it Iago.

IAGO: If you are so fond over her iniquity: give her patent to offend, for if it touch not you, it comes near nobody.

OTHELLO: I will chop her into messes: cuckold me?

IAGO: Oh, 'tis foul in her.

OTHELLO: With mine Officer?

IAGO: That 's fouler.

OTHELLO: Get me some poison, Iago, this night. I'll not expostulate with her: lest her body and beauty unprovide my mind again: this night Iago.

IAGO: Do it not with poison, strangle her in her bed,
Even the bed she hath contaminated.

OTHELLO: Good, good:
The justice of it pleases: very good.

IAGO: And for Cassio, let me be his undertaker:
You shall hear more by midnight.

A trumpet.

Enter Lodovico, Desdemona, and Attendants.

OTHELLO: Excellent good: What trumpet is that same?

IAGO: I warrant something from Venice,
'Tis Lodovico, this comes from the Duke.
See, your wife 's with him.

LODOVICO: God save you worthy General.

OTHELLO: With all my heart Sir.

LODOVICO: The Duke, and the Senators of Venice greet you.

OTHELLO: I kiss the instrument of their pleasures.

DESDEMONA: And what 's the news, good cousin Lodovico?

IAGO: I am very glad to see you Signior:
Welcome to Cyprus.

LODOVICO: I thank you: how does Lieutenant Cassio?

IAGO: Lives Sir.

DESDEMONA: Cousin, there 's fall'n between him, and my Lord,
An unkind breach: but you shall make all well.
OTHELLO: Are you sure of that?
DESDEMONA: My Lord?
OTHELLO: This fail you not to do, as you will —
LODOVICO: He did not call: he 's busy in the paper,
Is there division 'twixt my Lord, and Cassio?
DESDEMONA: A most unhappy one: I would do much
T' atone them, for the love I bear to Cassio.
OTHELLO: Fire, and brimstone.
DESDEMONA: My Lord.
OTHELLO: Are you wise?
DESDEMONA: What is he angry?
LODOVICO: May be th' letter mov'd him,
For as I think, they do command him home,
Deputing Cassio in his government.
DESDEMONA: By my troth, I am glad on 't.
OTHELLO: Indeed?
DESDEMONA: My Lord?
OTHELLO: I am glad to see you mad.
DESDEMONA: Why, sweet Othello?
OTHELLO: Devil.
DESDEMONA: I have not deserv'd this.
LODOVICO: My Lord, this would not be believ'd in Venice,
Though I should swear I saw't. 'Tis very much,
Make her amends: she weeps.
OTHELLO: Oh devil, devil:
If that the Earth could teem with women's tears,
Each drop she falls, would prove a crocodile:
Out of my sight.
DESDEMONA: I will not stay to offend you.
LODOVICO: Truly obedient Lady:
I do beseech your Lordship call her back.
OTHELLO: Mistress.
DESDEMONA: My Lord.

OTHELLO: What would you with her, Sir?
LODOVICO: Who I, my Lord?
OTHELLO: Ay, you did wish, that I would make her turn:
Sir, she can turn, and turn: and yet go on
And turn again. And she can weep, Sir, weep.
And she 's obedient: as you say obedient.
Very obedient: proceed you in your tears.
Concerning this Sir, (oh well-painted passion)
I am commanded home: get you away:
I'll send for you anon. Sir, I obey the mandate,
And will return to Venice. Hence, avaunt:
Exit Desdemona.
Cassio shall have my place. And Sir, tonight
I do entreat, that we may sup together.
You are welcome Sir, to Cyprus.
Goats, and monkeys. *Exit.*
LODOVICO: Is this the noble Moor, whom our full Senate
Call all in all sufficient? Is this the nature
Whom passion could not shake? Whose solid virtue
The shot of accident, nor dart of chance
Could neither graze, nor pierce?
IAGO: He is much chang'd.
LODOVICO: Are his wits safe? Is he not light of brain?
IAGO: He 's that he is: I may not breathe my censure.
What he might be: if what he might, he is not,
I would to heaven he were.
LODOVICO: What? Strike his wife?
IAGO: 'Faith that was not so well: yet would I knew
That stroke would prove the worst.
LODOVICO: Is it his use?
Or did the letters, work upon his blood,
And new create his fault?
IAGO: Alas, alas:
It is not honesty in me to speak
What I have seen, and known. You shall observe him,
And his own courses will denote him so,

That I may save my speech: do but go after
And mark how he continues.
LODOVICO: I am sorry that I am deceiv'd in him.
Exeunt.

IV.2

Enter Othello, and Emilia.

OTHELLO: You have seen nothing then?
EMILIA: Nor ever heard: nor ever did suspect.
OTHELLO: Yes, you have seen Cassio, and she together.
EMILIA: But then I saw no harm: and then I heard,
Each syllable that breath made up between them.
OTHELLO: What? Did they never whisper?
EMILIA: Never my Lord.
OTHELLO: Nor send you out o' th' way?
EMILIA: Never.
OTHELLO: To fetch her fan, her gloves, her mask, nor nothing?
EMILIA: Never my Lord.
OTHELLO: That 's strange.
EMILIA: I durst (my Lord) to wager, she is honest:
Lay down my soul at stake: If you think other,
Remove your thought. It doth abuse your bosom:
If any wretch have put this in your head,
Let Heaven requite it with the Serpent's curse,
For if she be not honest, chaste, and true,
There 's no man happy. The purest of their wives
Is foul as slander.
OTHELLO: Bid her come hither: go. *Exit Emilia.*
She says enough: yet she 's a simple bawd
That cannot say as much. This is a subtle whore:
A closet lock and key of villainous secrets,
And yet she'll kneel, and pray: I have seen her do 't.

Enter Desdemona, and Emilia.

DESDEMONA: My Lord, what is your will?

OTHELLO: Pray you Chuck come hither.

DESDEMONA: What is your pleasure?

OTHELLO: Let me see your eyes: look in my face.

DESDEMONA: What horrible fancy 's this?

OTHELLO: Some of your function Mistress:
Leave procreants alone, and shut the door:
Cough, or cry hem; if any body come:
Your mystery, your mystery: nay dispatch.

Exit Emilia.

DESDEMONA: Upon my knee, what doth your speech import?
I understand a fury in your words,
But not the words.

OTHELLO: Why? What art thou?

DESDEMONA: Your wife my Lord: your true and loyal wife.

OTHELLO: Come swear it: damn thyself, lest being like one of Heaven, the devils themselves should fear to seize thee.
Therefore be double-damn'd: swear thou art honest.

DESDEMONA: Heaven doth truly know it.

OTHELLO: Heaven truly knows, that thou art false as hell.

DESDEMONA: To whom my Lord?
With whom? How am I false?

OTHELLO: Ah Desdemon, away, away, away.

DESDEMONA: Alas the heavy day: why do you weep?
Am I the motive of these tears my Lord?
If happily you my Father do suspect,
An instrument of this your calling back,
Lay not your blame on me: if you have lost him,
I have lost him too.

OTHELLO: Had it pleas'd Heaven,
To try me with affliction, had they rain'd
All kinds of sores, and shames on my bare head:
Steep'd me in poverty to the very lips,
Given to captivity, me, and my utmost hopes,

I should have found in some place of my soul
A drop of patience. But alas, to make me
The fixed figure for the time of Scorn,
To point his slow, and moving finger at
Yet could I bear that too, well, very well:
But there where I have garner'd up my heart,
Where either I must live, or bear no life,
The fountain from the which my current runs,
Or else dries up: to be discarded thence,
Or keep it as a cistern, for foul toads
To knot and gender in. Turn thy complexion there:
Patience, thou young and rose-lipp'd cherubin,
I here look grim as hell.

DESDEMONA: I hope my noble Lord esteems me honest.

OTHELLO: Oh ay, as summer flies are in the shambles,
That quicken even with blowing. Oh thou weed:
Who art so lovely fair, and smell'st so sweet,
That the sense aches at thee,
Would thou hadst never been born.

DESDEMONA: Alas, what ignorant sin have I committed?

OTHELLO: Was this fair paper? This most goodly book
Made to write whore upon? What committed,
Committed? Oh, thou public commoner,
I should make very forges of my cheeks,
That would to cinders burn up modesty,
Did I but speak thy deeds. What committed?
Heaven stops the nose at it, and the Moon winks:
The bawdy wind that kisses all it meets,
Is hush'd within the hollow mine of Earth
And will not hear 't. What committed?
Impudent strumpet!

DESDEMONA: By Heaven you do me wrong.

OTHELLO: Are not you a strumpet?

DESDEMONA: No, as I am a Christian.
If to preserve this vessel for my Lord,
From any other foul unlawful touch

Be not to be a strumpet, I am none.
OTHELLO: What, not a whore?
DESDEMONA: No, as I shall be sav'd.
OTHELLO: Is 't possible?
DESDEMONA: Oh Heaven forgive us.
OTHELLO: I cry you mercy then.
I took you for that cunning whore of Venice,
That married with Othello. You Mistress,
Enter Emilia.
That have the office opposite to Saint Peter,
And keeps the gate of hell. You, you: ay you.
We have done our course: there 's money for your pains:
I pray you turn the key, and keep our counsel. *Exit.*
EMILIA: Alas, what does this Gentleman conceive?
How do you Madam? how do you my good Lady?
DESDEMONA: Faith, half asleep.
EMILIA: Good Madam,
What 's the matter with my Lord?
DESDEMONA: With who?
EMILIA: Why, with my Lord, Madam.
DESDEMONA: Who is thy Lord?
EMILIA: He that is yours, sweet Lady.
DESDEMONA: I have none: do not talk to me, Emilia,
I cannot weep: nor answers I have none,
But what should go by water. Prithee tonight,
Lay on my bed my wedding sheets, remember,
And call thy husband hither.
EMILIA: Here 's a change indeed. *Exit.*
DESDEMONA: 'Tis meet I should be us'd so: very meet.
How have I been behav'd, that he might stick
The small'st opinion on my least misuse?
Enter Iago and Emilia.
IAGO: What is your pleasure Madam?
How is 't with you?
DESDEMONA: I cannot tell: those that do teach young babes

Do it with gentle means, and easy tasks.
He might have chid me so: for in good faith
I am a child to chiding.
IAGO: What is the matter Lady?
EMILIA: Alas (Iago) my Lord hath so bewhor'd her,
Thrown such despite, and heavy terms upon her
That true heart cannot bear it.
DESDEMONA: Am I that name, Iago?
IAGO: What name (fair Lady)?
DESDEMONA: Such as she said my Lord did say I was.
EMILIA: He call'd her whore: a beggar in his drink
Could not have laid such terms upon his callet.
IAGO: Why did he so?
DESDEMONA: I do not know: I am sure I am none such.
IAGO: Do not weep, do not weep: alas the day.
EMILIA: Hath she forsook so many noble matches?
Her father? And her country? And her friends?
To be call'd whore? Would it not make one weep?
DESDEMONA: It is my wretched fortune.
IAGO: Beshrew him for 't:
How comes this trick upon him?
DESDEMONA: Nay, Heaven doth know.
EMILIA: I will be hang'd, if some eternal villain,
Some busy and insinuating rogue,
Some cogging, cozening slave, to get some office.
Have not devis'd this slander: I will be hang'd else.
IAGO: Fie, there is no such man: it is impossible.
DESDEMONA: If any such there be, Heaven pardon him.
EMILIA: A halter pardon him:
And hell gnaw his bones.
Why should he call her whore?
Who keeps her company?
What place? What time?
What form? What likelihood?
The Moor 's abus'd by some most villainous knave,
Some base notorious knave, some scurvy fellow.

Oh Heavens, that such companions thou 'ldst unfold.
And put in every honest hand a whip
To lash the rascals naked through the world,
Even from the East to th' West.

IAGO: Speak within door.

EMILIA: Oh fie upon them: some such squire he was
That turn'd your wit, the seamy side without,
And made you to suspect me with the Moor.

IAGO: You are a fool: go to.

DESDEMONA: Alas Iago,
What shall I do to win my Lord again?
Good friend, go to him: for by this light of Heaven,
I know not how I lost him. Here I kneel:
If e'er my will did trespass 'gainst his love,
Either in discourse of thought, or actual deed,
Or that mine eyes, mine ears, or any sense
Delighted them: or any other form.
Or that I do not yet, and ever did,
And ever will, (though he do shake me off
To beggarly divorcement) love him dearly,
Comfort forswear me. Unkindness may do much,
And his unkindness may defeat my life,
But never taint my love. I cannot say Whore,
It does abhor me now I speak the word,
To do the act, that might the addition earn,
Not the world's mass of vanity could make me.

IAGO: I pray you be content: 'tis but his humour.
The business of the State does him offence,
And he does chide with you.

DESDEMONA: If 'twere no other.

IAGO: It is but so, I varrant,
Hark how these instruments summon to supper:
And the messengers of Venice stays the meat,
Go in, and weep not: all things shall be well.

Exeunt Desdemona and Emilia,

Enter Roderigo.

How now Roderigo?

RODERIGO: I do not find
That thou deal'st justly with me.

IAGO: What in the contrary?

RODERIGO: Every day thou dafts me with some device Iago, and rather, as it seems to me now, keep'st from me all conveniency, than suppliest me with the least advantage of hope: I will indeed no longer endure it. Nor am I yet persuaded to put up in peace, what already I have foolishly suffer'd.

IAGO: Will you hear me Roderigo?

RODERIGO: Faith I have heard too much, for your words and performances are no kin together.

IAGO: You charge me most unjustly.

RODERIGO: With nought but truth: I have wasted myself out of my means. The jewels you have had from me to deliver Desdemona, would half have corrupted a votarist. You have told me she hath receiv'd them, and return'd me expectations and comforts of sudden respect, and acquaintance, but I find none.

IAGO: Well, go to: very well.

RODERIGO: Very well, go to: I cannot go to, (man) nor 'tis not very well. By this hand, I say it is scurvy: and begin to find myself fopp'd in it.

IAGO: Very well.

RODERIGO: I tell you, 'tis not very well: I will make myself known to Desdemona. If she will return me my jewels, I will give over my suit, and repent my unlawful solicitation. If not, assure yourself, I will seek satisfaction of you.

IAGO: You have said now.

RODERIGO: Ay: and said nothing but what I protest intendment of doing.

IAGO: Why, now I see there 's mettle in thee: and even from this instant do build on thee a better opinion than ever before: give me thy hand Roderigo. Thou hast taken against me a most just exception: but yet I protest I have dealt most directly in thy affair.

RODERIGO: It hath not appear'd.

IAGO: I grant indeed it hath not appear'd: and your suspicion is not without wit and judgement. But Roderigo, if thou hast that in thee indeed, which I have greater reason to believe now than ever (I mean purpose, courage, and valour) this night show it. If thou the next night following enjoy not Desdemona, take me from this world with treachery, and devise engines for my life.

RODERIGO: Well: what is it? Is it within reason and compass?

IAGO: Sir, there is especial Commission come from Venice to depute Cassio in Othello's place.

RODERIGO: Is that true? Why then Othello and Desdemona return again to Venice.

IAGO: Oh no: he goes into Mauritania and taketh away with him the fair Desdemona, unless his abode be linger'd here by some accident. Wherein none can be so determinate, as the removing of Cassio.

RODERIGO: How do you mean removing him?

IAGO: Why, by making him uncapable of Othello's place: knocking out his brains.

RODERIGO: And that you would have me to do.

IAGO: Ay: if you dare do yourself a profit, and a right. He sups tonight with a harlotry: and thither will I go to him. He knows not yet of his honourable fortune: if you will watch his going thence (which I will fashion to fall out between twelve and one) you may take him at your pleasure. I will near be to second your attempt, and he shall fall between us. Come, stand not amaz'd at it, but go along with me: I will show you such a necessity in his death, that you shall think yourself bound to put it on him. It is now high supper time: and the night grows to waste. About it.

RODERIGO: I will hear further reason for this.

IAGO: And you shall be satisfied.

Exeunt.

IV.3

Enter Othello, Lodovico, Desdemona, Emilia, and Attendants.

LODOVICO: I do beseech you Sir, trouble yourself no further.

OTHELLO: Oh pardon me: 'twill do me good to walk.

LODOVICO: Madam, good night: I humbly thank your Ladyship.

DESDEMONA: Your Honour is most welcome.

OTHELLO: Will you walk Sir? Oh Desdemona.

DESDEMONA: My Lord.

OTHELLO: Get you to bed on th' instant, I will be return'd forthwith: dismiss your attendant there: look 't be done.

Exeunt Othello, Lodovico, and Attendants.

DESDEMONA: I will my Lord.

EMILIA: How goes it now; He looks gentler than he did.

DESDEMONA: He says he will return incontinent,
And hath commanded me to go to bed,
And bid me to dismiss you.

EMILIA: Dismiss me?

DESDEMONA: It was his bidding: therefore good Emilia,
Give me my nightly wearing, and adieu.
We must not now displease him.

EMILIA: Ay, would you had never seen him.

DESDEMONA: So would not I: my love doth so approve him,
That even his stubbornness, his checks, his frowns,
(Prithee unpin me) have grace and favour.

EMILIA: I have laid those sheets you bade me on the bed.

DESDEMONA: All 's one: good Father, how foolish are our minds!
If I do die before, prithee shroud me
In one of these same sheets.

EMILIA: Come, come: you talk.
DESDEMONA: My Mother had a maid call'd Barbary,
She was in love: and he she lov'd prov'd mad,
And did forsake her. She had a song of willow,
An old thing 'twas: but it express'd her fortune,
And she died singing it. That song tonight,
Will not go from my mind: I have much to do,
But to go hang my head all at one side
And sing it like poor Barbary: prithee dispatch.
EMILIA: Shall I go fetch your night-gown?
DESDEMONA: No, unpin me here,
This Lodovico is a proper man.
EMILIA: A very handsome man.
DESDEMONA: He speaks well.
EMILIA: I know a Lady in Venice would have walk'd barefoot to Palestine for a touch of his nether lip.
DESDEMONA: *The poor soul sat sighing, by a sycamore tree.*
Sing all a green willow:
Her hand on her bosom, her head on her knee,
Sing willow, willow, willow.
The fresh streams ran by her, and murmur'd her moans,
Sing willow, &c.
Her salt tears fell from her, and soften'd the stones,
*Sing willow, &c. (*Lay by these*)*
*Willow, willow. (*Prithee hie thee: he'll come anon*)*
Sing all a green willow must be my garland,
Let nobody blame him, his scorn I approve.
(Nay that 's not next). Hark, who is 't that knocks?
EMILIA: It 's the wind.
DESDEMONA: *I call'd my Love false Love: but what said he then?*
Sing willow, &c.
If I court mo women, you'll couch with mo men.
So get thee gone, good night: mine eyes do itch:
Doth that bode weeping?
EMILIA: 'Tis neither here, nor there.

DESDEMONA: I have heard it said so. O these men, these men!
Dost thou in conscience think (tell me Emilia)
That there be women do abuse their husbands
In such gross kind?
EMILIA: There be some such, no question.
DESDEMONA: Wouldst thou do such a deed for all the world?
EMILIA: Why, would not you?
DESDEMONA: No, by this heavenly light.
EMILIA: Nor I neither, by this heavenly light:
I might do 't as well i' th' dark.
DESDEMONA: Wouldst thou do such a deed for all the world?
EMILIA: The world 's a huge thing:
It is a great price, for a small vice:
DESDEMONA: In troth, I think thou wouldst not.

EMILIA: In troth I think I should, and undo 't when I had done. Marry, I would not do such a thing for a joint ring, nor for measures of lawn, nor for gowns, petticoats, nor caps, nor any petty exhibition. But for all the whole world: 'uds pity, who would not make her husband a cuckold, to make him a Monarch? I should venture Purgatory for 't.

DESDEMONA: Beshrew me, if I would do such a wrong
For the whole world.

EMILIA: Why, the wrong is but a wrong i' th' world; and having the world for your labour, 'tis a wrong in your own world, and you might quickly make it right.

DESDEMONA: I do not think there is any such woman.

EMILIA: Yes, a dozen: and as many to th' vantage, as would store the world they play'd for.
But I do think it is their husbands' faults
If wives do fall: (Say, that they slack their duties,
And pour our treasuries into foreign laps;
Or else break out in peevish jealousies,
Throwing restraint upon us: Or say they strike us,
Or scant our former having in despite)
Why we have galls: and though we have some grace,
Yet have we some revenge. Let husbands know,

Their wives have sense like them: They see, and smell,
And have their palates both for sweet, and sour,
As husbands have. What is it that they do,
When they change us for others? Is it sport?
I think it is: and doth affection breed it?
I think it doth. Is 't frailty that thus errs?
It is so too. And have not we affections?
Desires for sport? and frailty, as men have?
Then let them use us well: else let them know,
The ills we do, their ills instruct us so.

DESDEMONA: Good night, good night:
Heaven me such uses send,
Not to pick bad, from bad; but by bad, mend.

Exeunt.

V.1

Enter Iago, and Roderigo.

IAGO: Here, stand behind this bulk,
Straight will he come:
Wear thy good rapier bare, and put it home:
Quick, quick, fear nothing; I'll be at thy elbow,
It makes us, or it mars us, think on that,
And fix most firm thy resolution.

RODERIGO: Be near at hand, I may miscarry in 't.

IAGO: Here, at thy hand: Be bold, and take thy stand.

RODERIGO: I have no great devotion to the deed,
And yet he hath given me satisfying reasons:
'Tis but a man gone. Forth my sword: he dies.

IAGO: I have rubb'd this young quat almost to the sense,
And he grows angry. Now, whether he kill Cassio,
Or Cassio him, or each do kill the other,

Every way makes my gain. Live Roderigo,
He calls me to a restitution large
Of gold, and jewels, that I bobb'd from him,
As gifts to Desdemona.
It must not be: If Cassio do remain,
He hath a daily beauty in his life,
That makes me ugly: and besides, the Moor
May unfold me to him: there stand I in much peril:
No, he must die. But so, I heard him coming.

Enter Cassio.

RODERIGO: I know his gait, 'tis he: villain thou diest.

CASSIO: That thrust had been mine enemy indeed,
But that my coat is better than thou know'st:
I will make proof of thine.

[*Stabs Roderigo.*]

RODERIGO: Oh, I am slain.

[*Iago wounds Cassio from behind: exit.*]

CASSIO: I am maim'd for ever:
Help hoa: murther, murther.

Enter Othello.

OTHELLO: The voice of Cassio, Iago keeps his word.

RODERIGO: O villain that I am.

OTHELLO: It is even so.

CASSIO: Oh help hoa: Light, a Surgeon.

OTHELLO: 'Tis he: O brave Iago, honest, and just,
That hast such noble sense of thy friend's wrong,
Thou teachest me. Minion, your dear lies dead,
And your unblest fate hies: Strumpet I come:
For of my heart, those charms thine eyes, are blotted:
Thy bed lust-stain'd, shall with lust's blood be spotted.

Exit Othello.

Enter Lodovico and Gratiano.

CASSIO: What hoa? no watch? No passage?
Murther, murther.

GRATIANO: 'Tis some mischance, the voice is very direful.

CASSIO: Oh help.

LODOVICO: Hark.

RODERIGO: Oh wretched villain.

LODOVICO: Two or three groan. 'Tis heavy night:
These may be counterfeits: Let 's think 't unsafe
To come into the cry, without more help.

RODERIGO: Nobody come: then shall I bleed to death.

Enter Iago.

LODOVICO: Hark.

GRATIANO: Here 's one comes in his shirt, with light, and weapons.

IAGO: Who 's there?
Whose noise is this that cries on murther?

LODOVICO: We do not know.

IAGO: Do not you hear a cry?

CASSIO: Here, here: for heaven' sake help me.

IAGO: What 's the matter?

GRATIANO: This is Othello's Ancient, as I take it.

LODOVICO: The same indeed, a very valiant fellow.

IAGO: What are you here, that cry so grievously?

CASSIO: Iago? Oh I am spoil'd, undone by villains:
Give me some help.

IAGO: O me, Lieutenant!
What villains have done this?

CASSIO: I think that one of them is hereabout,
And cannot make away.

IAGO: Oh treacherous villains:
What are you there? Come in, and give some help.

RODERIGO: O help me here.

CASSIO: That 's one of them.

IAGO: Oh murd'rous slave! O villain! [*Stabs Roderigo.*]

RODERIGO: O damn'd Iago! O inhuman dog!

IAGO: Kill men i' th' dark?
Where be these bloody thieves?
How silent is this town! Hoa, murther, murther.
What may you be? Are you of good, or evil?

LODOVICO: As you shall prove us, praise us.

IAGO: Signior Lodovico?
LODOVICO: He sir.
IAGO: I cry you mercy: here 's Cassio hurt by villains.
GRATIANO: Cassio?
IAGO: How is 't Brother?
CASSIO: My leg is cut in two.
IAGO: Marry heaven forbid:
Light gentlemen, I'll bind it with my shirt.

Enter Bianca.

BIANCA: What is the matter hoa? Who is 't that cried?
IAGO: Who is 't that cried?
BIANCA: Oh my dear Cassio,
My sweet Cassio: Oh Cassio, Cassio, Cassio.
IAGO: O notable strumpet. Cassio, may you suspect
Who they should be, that have thus mangled you?
CASSIO: No.
GRATIANO: I am sorry to find you thus;
I have been to seek you.
IAGO: Lend me a garter. So: – Oh for a chair.
To bear him easily hence.
BIANCA: Alas he faints. Oh, Cassio, Cassio, Cassio.
IAGO: Gentlemen all, I do suspect this trash
To be a party in this injury.
Patience awhile, good Cassio. Come, come;
Lend me a light: know we this face, or no?
Alas my friend, and my dear countryman
Roderigo? No: Yes sure: Yes, 'tis Roderigo.
GRATIANO: What, of Venice?
IAGO: Even he sir: Did you know him?
GRATIANO: Know him? Ay.
IAGO: Signior Gratiano? I cry your gentle pardon:
These bloody accidents must excuse my manners,
That so neglected you.
GRATIANO: I am glad to see you.

IAGO: How do you Cassio? Oh, a chair, a chair.
[*Enter some with a chair.*]
GRATIANO: Roderigo?
IAGO: He, he, 'tis he:
Oh that 's well said, the chair.
Some good man bear him carefully from hence,
I'll fetch the General's surgeon. For you Mistress,
Save you your labour. He that lies slain here (Cassio)
Was my dear friend. What malice was between you?
CASSIO: None in the world: nor do I know the man.
IAGO: What? look you pale? Oh bear him out o' th' air.
Stay you good Gentlemen. Look you pale, Mistress?
Do you perceive the gastness of her eye?
Nay, if you stare, we shall hear more anon.
Behold her well: I pray you look upon her:
Do you see Gentlemen? Nay, guiltiness will speak
Though tongues were out of use.
Enter Emilia.
EMILIA: Alas, what is the matter?
What is the matter, husband?
IAGO: Cassio hath here been set on in the dark
By Roderigo, and fellows that are 'scap'd:
He's almost slain, and Roderigo quite dead.
EMILIA: Alas good Gentleman: alas good Cassio.
IAGO: This is the fruits of whoring. Prithee Emilia,
Go know of Cassio where he supp'd tonight.
What, do you shake at that?
BIANCA: He supp'd at my house, but I therefore shake not.
IAGO: O did he so? I charge you go with me.
EMILIA: Oh fie upon thee strumpet.
BIANCA: I am no strumpet, but of life as honest,
As you that thus abuse me.
EMILIA: As I? Fie upon thee.
IAGO: Kind Gentlemen:

Let 's go see poor Cassio dress'd.
Come Mistress, you must tell 's another tale.
Emilia, run you to the Citadel,
And tell my Lord and Lady, what hath happ'd:
Will you go on afore? This is the night
That either makes me, or fordoes me quite.

Exeunt.

V.2

Enter Othello with a light: Desdemona in her bed.

OTHELLO: It is the cause, it is the cause (my soul)
Let me not name it to you, you chaste Stars,
It is the cause. Yet I'll not shed her blood,
Nor scar that whiter skin of hers, than snow,
And smooth as monumental alablaster:
Yet she must die, else she'll betray more men:
Put out the light, and then put out the light:
If I quench thee, thou flaming minister,
I can again thy former light restore,
Should I repent me. But once put out thy light,
Thou cunning'st pattern of excelling Nature,
I know not where is that Promethean heat
That can thy light re-lume.
When I have pluck'd thy rose,
I cannot give it vital growth again,
It needs must wither. I'll smell thee on the tree.
Oh balmy breath, that dost almost persuade
Justice to break her sword. One more, one more:
Be thus when thou art dead, and I will kill thee,
And love thee after. One more, and that's the last.

So sweet, was ne'er so fatal. I must weep,
But they are cruel tears: This sorrow 's heavenly,
It strikes, where it doth love. She wakes.
DESDEMONA: Who 's there? Othello?
OTHELLO: Ay Desdemona.
DESDEMONA: Will you come to bed, my Lord?
OTHELLO: Have you pray'd tonight, Desdemona?
DESDEMONA: Ay my Lord.
OTHELLO: If you bethink yourself of any crime
Unreconcil'd as yet to Heaven, and Grace,
Solicit for it straight.
DESDEMONA: Alack, my Lord,
What may you mean by that?
OTHELLO: Well, do it, and be brief, I will walk by:
I would not kill thy unprepared spirit,
No, Heavens forfend, I would not kill thy soul.
DESDEMONA: Talk you of killing?
OTHELLO: Ay, I do.
DESDEMONA: Then Heaven have mercy on me.
OTHELLO: Amen, with all my heart.
DESDEMONA: If you say so, I hope you will not kill me.
OTHELLO: Humh.
DESDEMONA: And yet I fear you: for you are fatal then
When your eyes roll so.
Why I should fear, I know not,
Since guiltiness I know not: But yet I feel I fear.
OTHELLO: Think on thy sins.
DESDEMONA: They are loves I bear to you.
OTHELLO: Ay, and for that thou diest.
DESDEMONA: That death 's unnatural, that kills for loving.
Alas, why gnaw you so your nether-lip?
Some bloody passion shakes your very frame:
These are portents: but yet I hope, I hope,
They do not point on me.
OTHELLO: Peace, and be still.

DESDEMONA: I will so: What 's the matter?
OTHELLO: That handkerchief
Which I so lov'd, and gave thee, thou gav'st to Cassio.
DESDEMONA: No by my life, and soul: send for the man,
And ask him.
OTHELLO: Sweet soul, take heed, take heed of perjury,
Thou art on thy death-bed.
DESDEMONA: Ay, but not yet to die.
OTHELLO: Presently.
Therefore confess thee freely of thy sin:
For to deny each article with oath,
Cannot remove, nor choke the strong conception
That I do groan withal. Thou art to die.
DESDEMONA: O Heaven have mercy on me.
OTHELLO: I say, Amen.
DESDEMONA: And have you mercy too. I never did
Offend you in my life: never lov'd Cassio,
But with such general warranty of Heaven,
As I might love. I never gave him token.
OTHELLO: By Heaven I saw my handkerchief in 's hand.
O perjur'd woman, thou dost stone my heart,
And makes me call, what I intend to do,
A murther, which I thought a sacrifice.
I saw the handkerchief.
DESDEMONA: He found it then:
I never gave it him: Send, for him hither:
Let him confess a truth.
OTHELLO: He hath confess'd.
DESDEMONA: What, my Lord?
OTHELLO: That he hath us'd thee.
DESDEMONA: How? unlawfully?
OTHELLO: Ay.
DESDEMONA: He will not say so.
OTHELLO: No: his mouth is stopp'd:
Honest Iago hath ta'en order for 't.

DESDEMONA: Oh, my fear interprets. What is he dead?

OTHELLO: Had all his hairs been lives, my great revenge Had
stomach for them all.

DESDEMONA: Alas, he is betray'd, and I undone.

OTHELLO: Out strumpet: weep'st thou for him to my face?

DESDEMONA: O banish me, my Lord, but kill me not.

OTHELLO: Down strumpet.

DESDEMONA: Kill me tomorrow, let me live tonight.

OTHELLO: Nay, if you strive.

DESDEMONA: But half an hour.

OTHELLO: Being done, there is no pause.

DESDEMONA: But while I say one prayer.

OTHELLO: It is too late. *Smothers her.*

Emilia calls at the door.

EMILIA: My Lord, my Lord? What hoa?
My Lord, my Lord.

OTHELLO: What noise is this? Not dead? not yet quite dead?
I that am cruel, am yet merciful,
I would not have thee linger in thy pain.
So, so.

EMILIA *within:* What hoa? My Lord, my Lord?

OTHELLO: Who 's there?

EMILIA: Oh good my Lord, I would speak a word with you.

OTHELLO: Yes: 'Tis Emilia: by and by. She 's dead.
'Tis like she comes to speak of Cassio's death:
The noise was high. Hah, no more moving?
Still as the grave. Shall she come in? Were 't good?
I think she stirs again. No, what 's best to do?
If she come in, she'll sure speak to my wife:
My wife, my wife: what wife? I have no wife.
Oh insupportable! Oh heavy hour!
Methinks, it should be now a huge eclipse
Of Sun, and Moon; and that th' affrighted Globe
Did yawn at alteration.

EMILIA: I do beseech you
That I may speak with you. Good my Lord.

OTHELLO: I had forgot thee: oh, come in Emilia.
Soft, by and by, let me the curtains draw.
Where art thou? What 's the matter with thee now?

Enter Emilia.

EMILIA: Oh my good Lord, yonder 's foul murthers done.
OTHELLO: What? now?
EMILIA: But now, my Lord.
OTHELLO: It is the very error of the Moon,
She comes more nearer Earth than she was wont,
And makes men mad.
EMILIA: Cassio, my Lord, hath kill'd
A young Venetian, call'd Roderigo.
OTHELLO: Roderigo kill'd? and Cassio kill'd?
EMILIA: No, Cassio is not kill'd.
OTHELLO: Not Cassio kill'd? Then murther 's out of tune,
And sweet revenge grows harsh.
DESDEMONA: O falsely, falsely murder'd.
EMILIA: Alas! what cry is that?
OTHELLO: That? What?
EMILIA: Out and alas, that was my Lady's voice.
Help, help hoa, help. Oh Lady speak again,
Sweet Desdemona, oh sweet Mistress, speak.
DESDEMONA: A guiltless death, I die,
EMILIA: Oh who hath done this deed?
DESDEMONA: Nobody: I myself, farewell:
Commend me to my kind Lord: oh farewell. *She dies.*
OTHELLO: Why, how should she be murder'd?
EMILIA: Alas: who knows?
OTHELLO: You hear her say herself, it was not I.
EMILIA: She said so: I must needs report the truth.
OTHELLO: She's like a liar gone to burning hell,
'Twas I that kill'd her.
EMILIA: Oh me more Angel she, and you the blacker Devil.
OTHELLO: She turn'd to folly: and she was a whore.
EMILIA: Thou dost belie her, and thou art a devil.
OTHELLO: She was false as water.

EMILIA: Thou art rash as fire, to say
 That she was false. Oh she was heavenly true.
OTHELLO: Cassio did top her: Ask thy husband else.
 O, I were damn'd beneath all depth in hell:
 But that I did proceed upon just grounds
 To this extremity. Thy husband knew it all.
EMILIA: My husband?
OTHELLO: Thy husband.
EMILIA: That she was false to wedlock?
OTHELLO: Ay, with Cassio: had she been true,
 If Heaven would make me such another world,
 Of one entire and perfect chrysolite,
 I 'ed not have sold her for it.
EMILIA: My husband?
OTHELLO: Ay, 'twas he that told me on her first.
 An honest man he is, and hates the slime
 That sticks on filthy deeds.
EMILIA: My husband?
OTHELLO: What needs this iterance, woman?
 I say, thy husband.
EMILIA: Oh Mistress,
 Villainy hath made mocks with love:
 My husband say she was false?
OTHELLO: He, woman;
 I say thy husband: Dost understand the word?
 My friend, thy husband; honest, honest Iago.
EMILIA: If he say so, may his pernicious soul
 Rot half a grain a day: he lies to th' heart,
 She was too fond of her most filthy bargain.
OTHELLO: Hah?
EMILIA: Do thy worst:
 This deed of thine is no more worthy Heaven,
 Than thou wast worthy her.
OTHELLO: Peace, you were best.
EMILIA: Thou hast not half that power to do me harm,
 As I have to be hurt. Oh gull, oh dolt,

As ignorant as dirt: thou hast done a deed
(I care not for thy sword) I'll make thee known,
Though I lost twenty lives. Help, help, hoa, help:
The Moor hath kill'd my Mistress. Murther, murther.

Enter Montano, Gratiano, and Iago.

MONTANO: What is the matter? How now General?
EMILIA: Oh, are you come, Iago: you have done well,
That men must lay their murthers on your neck.
GRATIANO: What is the matter?
EMILIA: Disprove this villain, if thou be'st a man:
He says, thou told'st him that his wife was false:
I know thou didst not: thou 'rt not such a villain.
Speak, for my heart is full.
IAGO: I told him what I thought,
And told no more
Than what he found himself was apt, and true.
EMILIA: But did you ever tell him,
She was false?
IAGO: I did.
EMILIA: You told a lie, an odious damned lie:
Upon my soul, a lie; a wicked lie.
She false with Cassio?
Did you say with Cassio?
IAGO: With Cassio, Mistress!
Go to, charm your tongue.
EMILIA: I will not charm my tongue;
I am bound to speak,
My Mistress here lies murthered in her bed.
ALL: Oh Heavens, forfend.
EMILIA: And your reports have set the murder on.
OTHELLO: Nay sure not Masters,
It is true indeed.
GRATIANO: 'Tis a strange truth.
MONTANO: O monstrous act.
EMILIA: Villainy, villainy, villainy:
I think upon 't, I think: I smell 't: O villainy:

I thought so then: I'll kill myself for grief.
O villainy! villainy!

IAGO: What, are you mad?
I charge you get you home.

EMILIA: Good Gentlemen, let me have leave to speak:
'Tis proper I obey him: but not now:
Perchance Iago, I will ne'er go home.

Othello falls on the bed.

OTHELLO: Oh, oh, oh.

EMILIA: Nay, lay thee down, and roar:
For thou hast kill'd the sweetest innocent,
That e'er did lift up eye.

OTHELLO: Oh she was foul!
I scarce did know you Uncle, there lies your niece,
Whose breath (indeed) these hands have newly stopp'd:
I know this act shows horrible and grim.

GRATIANO: Poor Desdemon:
I am glad thy Father 's dead,
Thy match was mortal to him: and pure grief
Shore his old thread in twain. Did he live now,
This sight would make him do a desperate turn:
Yea, curse his better Angel from his side,
And fall to reprobance.

OTHELLO: 'Tis pitiful: but yet Iago knows
That she with Cassio, hath the act of shame,
A thousand times committed. Cassio confess'd it,
And she did gratify his amorous works
With that recognizance and pledge of love
Which I first gave her: I saw it in his hand:
It was a handkerchief, an antique token
My Father gave my Mother.

EMILIA: Oh God! heavenly God!

IAGO: 'Zounds, hold your peace.

EMILIA: 'Twill out, 'twill out. I peace?
No, I will speak as liberal as the North;
Let Heaven, and men, and devils, let them all,

All, all, cry shame against me, yet I'll speak.
IAGO: Be wise, and get you home.
EMILIA: I will not.
GRATIANO: Fie, Your sword upon a woman.
EMILIA: Oh thou dull Moor,
That handkerchief thou speak'st of
I found by fortune, and did give my husband:
For often, with a solemn earnestness,
(More than indeed belong'd to such a trifle)
He begg'd of me, to steal 't.
IAGO: Villainous whore.
EMILIA: She give it Cassio? No, alas I found it,
And I did give 't my husband.
IAGO: Filth, thou liest.
EMILIA: By Heaven I do not, I do not Gentlemen:
Oh murd'rous coxcomb, what should such a fool
Do with so good a wife?
OTHELLO: Are there no stones in Heaven,
But what serves for the thunder?
Precious villain.
[*The Moor runs at Iago. Iago kills his wife.*]
GRATIANO: The woman falls:
Sure he hath kill'd his wife.
Exit Iago
EMILIA: Ay, ay: oh lay me by my Mistress' side.
GRATIANO: He 's gone, but his wife 's kill'd.
MONTANO: 'Tis a notorious villain: take you this weapon
Which I have here recover'd from the Moor:
Come guard the door without, let him not pass,
But kill him rather. I'll after that same villain,
For 'tis a damned slave.
Exit.
OTHELLO: I am not valiant neither:
But every puny whipster gets my sword.
But why should honour outlive honesty?
Let it go all.

EMILIA: What did thy song bode Lady?
Hark, canst thou hear me? I will play the swan,
And die in music: *Willow, willow, willow.*
Moor, she was chaste: She lov'd thee, cruel Moor,
So come my soul to bliss, as I speak true:
So speaking as I think, alas, I die. *She dies.*
OTHELLO: I have another weapon in this chamber,
It was a sword of Spain, the ice brook's temper:
Oh here it is: Uncle I must come forth.
GRATIANO: If thou attempt it, it will cost thee dear;
Thou hast no weapon, and perforce must suffer.
OTHELLO: Look in upon me then, and speak with me,
Or naked as I am I will assault thee.
GRATIANO: What is the matter?
OTHELLO: Behold, I have a weapon:
A better never did itself sustain
Upon a soldier's thigh. I have seen the day,
That with this little arm, and this good sword,
I have made my way through more impediments
Than twenty times your stop. But (oh vain boast)
Who can control his Fate? 'Tis not so now.
Be not afraid, though you do see me weapon'd:
Here is my journey's end, here is my butt
And very sea-mark of my utmost sail.
Do you go back dismay'd? 'Tis a lost fear:
Man but a rush against Othello's breast,
And he retires. Where should Othello go?
Now: how dost thou look now? Oh ill-starr'd wench,
Pale as thy smock: when we shall meet at compt,
This looks of thine will hurl my soul from Heaven,
And fiends will snatch at it. Cold, cold, my girl?
Even like thy chastity. O cursed, cursed slave!
Whip me ye devils
From the possession of this heavenly sight:
Blow me about in winds, roast me in sulphur,
Wash me in steep-down gulfs of liquid fire:

Oh Desdemon! dead Desdemon: dead. Oh, oh!

Enter Lodovico, Montano, Iago, and Officers: Cassio in a chair.

LODOVICO: Where is this rash, and most unfortunate man?

OTHELLO: That 's he that was Othello: here I am.

LODOVICO: Where is that viper?
Bring the villain forth.

OTHELLO: I look down towards his feet; but that 's a fable,
If that thou be'st a Devil, I cannot kill thee.

LODOVICO: Wrench his sword from him.

IAGO: I bleed Sir, but not kill'd.

OTHELLO: I am not sorry neither, I'ld have thee live:
For in my sense, 'tis happiness to die.

LODOVICO: Oh thou Othello, that was once so good,
Fall'n in the practice of a cursed slave,
What shall be said to thee.

OTHELLO: Why any thing:
An honourable murderer, if you will:
For nought I did in hate, but all in honour.

LODOVICO: This wretch hath part confess'd his villainy:
Did you and he consent in Cassio's death.

OTHELLO: Ay.

CASSIO: Dear General, I never gave you cause.

OTHELLO: I do believe it, and I ask your pardon:
Will you, I pray, demand that demi-devil,
Why he hath thus ensnar'd my soul and body?

IAGO: Demand me nothing: what you know, you know:
From this time forth, I never will speak word.

LODOVICO: What? not to pray?

GRATIANO: Torments will ope your lips.

OTHELLO: Well, thou dost best.

LODOVICO: Sir,
You shall understand what hath befall'n,
(Which, as I think, you know not) here is a letter
Found in the pocket of the slain Roderigo,
And here another, the one of them imports

The death of Cassio, to be undertook
By Roderigo.
OTHELLO: O villain!
CASSIO: Most heathenish, and most gross.
LODOVICO: Now, here 's another discontented paper
Found in his pocket too: and this it seems,
Roderigo meant t' have sent this damned villain:
But that (belike) Iago in the interim
Came in, and satisfied him.
OTHELLO: Oh thou pernicious caitiff;
How came you (Cassio) by that handkerchief
That was my wife's?
CASSIO: I found it in my chamber:
And he himself confess'd it but even now,
That there he dropp'd it for a special purpose,
Which wrought to his desire.
OTHELLO: O fool, fool, fool!
CASSIO: There is besides, in Roderigo's letter,
How he upbraids Iago, that he made him
Brave me upon the watch: whereon it came
That I was cast: and even but now he spake
(After long seeming dead) Iago hurt him,
Iago set him on.
LODOVICO: You must forsake this room, and go with us:
Your power, and your command is taken off,
And Cassio rules in Cyprus. For this slave,
If there be any cunning cruelty,
That can torment him much, and hold him long,
It shall be his. You shall close prisoner rest,
Till that the nature of your fault be known
To the Venetian State. Come, bring away.
OTHELLO: Soft you; a word or two before you go:
I have done the State some service, and they know 't:
No more of that. I pray you in your letters,
When you shall these unlucky deeds relate,
Speak of me, as I am. Nothing extenuate,

Nor set down aught in malice.
Then you must speak,
Of one that lov'd not wisely, but too well:
Of one, not easily jealous, but being wrought,
Perplex'd in the extreme: Of one, whose hand
(Like the base Indian) threw a pearl away
Richer than all his tribe: Of one, whose subdu'd eyes,
Albeit unused to the melting mood,
Drops tears as fast as the Arabian trees
Their medicinable gum. Set you down this:
And say besides, that in Aleppo once,
Where a malignant, and a turban'd Turk
Beat a Venetian, and traduc'd the State,
I took by th' throat the circumcised dog,
And smote him, thus.

He stabs himself.

LODOVICO: Oh bloody period.

GRATIANO: All that is spoke, is marr'd.

OTHELLO: I kiss'd thee, ere I kill'd thee: No way but this
Killing myself, to die upon a kiss. *Dies.*

CASSIO: This did I fear, but thought he had no weapon:
For he was great of heart.

LODOVICO: Oh Spartan dog:
More fell than anguish, hunger, or the sea:
Look on the tragic loading of this bed:
This is thy work:
The object poisons sight,
Let it be hid. Gratiano, keep the house,
And seize upon the fortunes of the Moor,
For they succeed on you. To you, Lord Governor,
Remains the censure of this hellish villain:
The time, the place, the torture, oh inforce it:
Myself will straight aboard, and to the State,
This heavy act, with heavy heart relate.

Exeunt.

GLOSSARY

addition: title
advantage: opportunity
advocation: advocacy
affined: bound by a tie of affection
affinity: kindred
agnize: acknowledge
alteration: portentous change
amiable: loved
ancient: ensign, 2nd lieutenant
anon: directly, soon
Anthropophagi: cannibals
antres: caves
approved: proved guilty
arraigning: accusing
arrivance: arrivals, news
assay: test
atone: reconcile
attach: arrest

bauble: worthless trifle
beshrew: ill luck to
besort: proper attendants
blazoning: describing, praising
bobb'd: cheated
boding: causing foreboding
bolster: sleep together
brace: defence
bridal: wedding day
bulk: stall
butt: aim

cable: rope
caitiff: wretch
callet: drab
capable: capacious
cast: dismissed
censure: judgement
charter: privilege
check: reprimand
choler: wrath
chrysolite: jasper
circumstanc'd: put off with excuses
clip: embrace
clyster-pipes: enemas
coffers: trunks
cogging: lying
collied: made dark
coloquintida: bitter cucumber
commission: official instructions
companions: low fellows
composition: agreement
conceit: thought, idea

conceits: thinks, imagines
conception: imaginary notion
conduct: escort
conserve: distil, interpret
continuate: uninterrupted
cope: encounter
counterfeits: fakers
cozening: cheating
customer: prostitute

daff: push aside, put off
dam: mother
dear: touching closely
defeat: destroy
displeasure: lack of favour
disports: pleasures
distempering: intoxicating
doubt: suspect, suspicion
Diablo: the devil

ecstasy: violent emotion
Egyptian: gipsy
embay'd: anchored
encave: conceal
enchafed: enraged
engender'd: conceived
engluts: swallows greedily
engines: instruments of torture
ensteep'd: submerged
exhibition: allowance, reward
expectancy: hope

fadom: depth, experience
fain: gladly
favour: face
fear: frighten
fig's end: trifle
fitchew: polecat
fleers: scornful grins
flag: sign of welcome
fond: foolish
footing: arrival
fopp'd: fooled
for: because
forc'd: unnatural
forfend: forbid
fraught: freight, cargo
freeze: coarse cloth with a nap
full: complete
function: intelligence, trade
fustian: coarse cloth, nonsense

galls: tempers
gastness: terror
gender: kind
generous: noble
germans: relations
get: beget
government: self-control
grange: lonely farm
grief: suffering, pain
gripe: grip
grise: step
guardage: guardianship
gutter'd: worn into channels
gyve: fetter, ensnare

haggard: wild hawk
harlotry: harlot
hearted: heartfelt

hies: hastens
hobby-horse: low companion
housewife: hussy
humour: whim
Hydra: a many-head monster killed by Hercules

idle: waste
import: concern
incontinent: forthwith
incorporate: bodily
indign: unworthy
indirect: underhand
indues: brings to
injointed: united
ingraffed: ingrained
inhibited: prohibited
innovation: revolution
intentively: carefully

joint-ring: ring made in two pieces
jump: (1) agree; (2) exactly
just: exact

latest: last
lawn: fine linen
lay: bet, wager
learn: teach
letter: private recommendation
lown: lout

mamm'ring: hesitating
mandragora: a soporific root
match: compare
mazzard: head
medicines: love potions
mere: sheer, utter
minerals: poisonous drugs
minister: servant
moe: more
molestation: turmoil
mortal: deadly
motion: will power
mummy: concoction made from Egyptian mummies
mystery: business

nether: lower

offices: i.e., the kitchens
owe: own, possess

paddle: play lovingly
pagans: heathens
pageant: show
paragons: equals in perfection
parcels: portions
passing: exceedingly
peculiar: one's own
period: conclusion
pith: marrow
poise: counterbalance
parlance: bearing
practise: plot
prefer: charge
pregnant: probable
prerogativ'd: privileged
present: immediate
prick'd: spurred

prime: eager
probal: probable
probation: proof
producted: produced as witness
profit: gain of experience
proper: (1) handsome; (2) own
propriety: natural condition
purse: draw together

qualified: mixed
qualification: allaying
quat: pimple
quicken: first have life
quillets: verbal subtleties
quirks: witty sayings, phrases

recognizance: token
remorse: (1) pity; (2) solemn obligation
repeals: recalls
reprobation: damnation
re-stem: turn back
rheum: moisture, a cold
rites: intercourse
rouse: a deep drink

salt: lustful
sans: without
'Sblood: by God's blood
scattering: casual
scored: marked as with a whip lash
secure: careless, carefree
seel: make blind
seeming: pretence
segregation: separation
self-bounty: natural goodness
sennight: week
sense: interpretation
sequent: following
sequester: separation
shrift: place for confession
Sibyl: prophetess
sith: since
skillet: saucepan
slipper: slippery
slubber: tarnish
snipe: woodcock, fool
spleen: passion of anger
stead: aid
still: always
stillness: staid behaviour
stone: turn to stone
stoup: pot holding two quarts
suppli'd: filled up

tainting: disparaging
taper: candle
teem: breed
thrice-driven: triply refined
timorous: terrifying
traverse: quick march
tupping: covering
Turk: heathen

'uds: God's
unbitted: unbridled
unbookish: simple minded

unfold: expose
unfolding: plan
unhoused: free
unlace: undo
unproper: not their own, shared

venial: pardonable
voices: votes, agreement

wage: risk
whipster: whipper-snapper
wight: creature
wrack: wreck

yerk'd: jerked, struck
yoked: married

'*Zounds*: by God's wounds